# Contents

# *Preface*

Effective schools have always striven to provide appropriate learning environments. All schools are now required to meet this challenge, to demonstrate accountability, and consequently have become more aware of 'image'. A major component of good 'image' is the maintenance of an ordered atmosphere. Simultaneously, we have seen a gradual increase in emphasis on children's rights in all spheres of our lives. In response to this and to recent legislation, schools have been increasingly involved in developing policies which relate to social aspects of the educational context. Most schools today have a code of conduct which describes how an orderly atmosphere can be achieved; an equal opportunity policy which aims to challenge prejudice and discrimination; an anti-bullying policy which proposes solutions to aggressive and hostile incidents and a special needs policy which sets out how children with special educational needs will be integrated into a mainstream setting. Sometimes these policies are seen as separate entities – discrete aspects of social behaviour. In this book we propose that all of these areas, whilst retaining specific and unique features, are inextricably linked by management procedures with the common aim of enhancing constructive relationships.

Whether primary or secondary, the key to successful policy development for these areas relies upon a definable process. This book sets out to describe and discuss the nature of this process.

# CHAPTER 1

# Why Whole School Policies?

## Introduction – the school as a community

This book describes some of the reasons why children often behave in a less than ideal way in school, particularly why they bully each other, exclude each other from groups, and set up long term antagonisms. It also goes on to describe some of the ways in which schools can set up policies to reduce the amount of bullying, racism, and social exclusion of children with special needs, and can integrate these policies together over a period of time to maintain their effectiveness. Some educationists have had great doubts as to whether such things as whole school behaviour policies can actually exist in any meaningful way, let alone have any effect, but recent research into the prevention of bullying has convincingly demonstrated that they do exist, and can have quite marked effects if they are implemented in certain ways.

A major problem schools face in dealing with any examples of long term aggressive behaviour is that the behaviour does not only exist in the particular incidents which are picked up, but the attitudes which lead to that behaviour are widespread amongst groups of children. To influence behaviour generally across the school, key values and expectations of appropriate standards of behaviour have to be identified in each area of concern by as many people in the school community as possible. Any one person would find it a daunting, if not impossible task, to pin down expected standards of behaviour for all the situations where they need to be emphasised, but the task becomes much easier if the insights and energies of both children and staff are involved.

Order and 'discipline' in schools are always of concern to school staff and the wider community. Commenting publicly guarantees any speaker the tabloid headlines. The Elton Report (1989) said that 'all children were entitled to a safe and ordered learning environment'. Whole school behaviour policies, thoroughly devised and implemented, give one of the most

effective sets of procedures to achieve such an orderly learning environment. 'School rules' tend to concentrate on issues important for the adults
in school, and unless widened considerably to include children's priorities
and children's voices in their formulation and implementation, they will
continue to be seen by children as of dubious relevance to their lives.

## The integration of separate behaviour policies

Many schools have developed positive behaviour policies following the
general discussion of the Elton Report and the evolution of in-service
training packages on behaviour management themes (Galvin, Mercer and
Costa, 1989). These describe how schools can use consultation with the
children and all the school staff to devise necessary rules and principles
which contribute to school being an orderly and supportive place. These
efforts are sometimes supported by their Local Education Authority
through policy initiatives and sometimes led by them. If we examine the
different kinds of policies relating to the management of behaviour we can
see that they fall broadly into two groups. The first group could be classed
as 'organisational' behaviour policies. These kinds of policies concern
themselves mainly with the smooth running of the school and commonly
describe how students should move around the school, procedures for the
completion of homework, school responses to lateness, dress requirements, health and safety issues and the promotion of effective study skills.
The second group of behaviour policies relate more to the development
and maintenance of constructive relationships between members of the
school community. They specify expectations of interactions between students and staff and are usually firmly grounded upon a philosophy of equal
opportunities. Included in this group of policies are those which concern
themselves with challenging racism, sexism and bullying behaviour and
about how students with special educational needs can be socially integrated into a mainstream setting.

## Victimisation, rejection and discrimination

Most kinds of victimisation and rejection are based upon negative discrimination of one kind or another. Prejudice and harassment involve discriminat-
ing or aggressive behaviour against an individual because of their perceived
membership of a particular group. These kinds of behaviours constitute an
attack on a person's identity – it occurs because of negative discrimination
against a particular gender, race, culture or disability. Bullying behaviour is
more often an attack against someone's individuality. It reflects negative discrimination at a more personal level and may relate to a distinguishing feature, mannerism or relationship. Discrimination, then, is the linking feature of
the different kinds of behaviours discussed in this and other chapters.

It is because of this common feature that we suggest the need for integrated behaviour policies which view these kinds of behaviours as a continuum and provide a cohesive approach to response and prevention. Whether aiming to tackle racism, sexism, bullying or harassment and rejection of students with special education needs, the core principle of any behaviour policy will be to challenge negative discrimination and to promote constructive relationship skills.

The current book has arisen out of evaluation of the operation of the whole school anti-bullying policies in a recent large scale Department for Education sponsored research project in Sheffield, and in particular from the insights gained into the co-ordination between all these separate types of whole school behaviour policies. If they are planned together as parts of a general, management supported whole school behaviour policy initiative, they can reinforce each other and make the task of maintaining the policy over time much easier. If they are left to evolve as separate initiatives, there is a danger that each of them will be less well established in the first place and become less effective over time.

## Why the 'behaviour' in Whole School Behaviour Policies?

All the policy areas mentioned above have implications for the organisation and resourcing of educational provision, and for the attitudes and behaviour of all members of the school community. In many ways the organisation of the provision is the first question for the school system and individual schools to address. Many of the arguments and changes over the past decades have posed questions about the best form of educational arrangements to educate girls as opposed to boys, children who make normal progress as opposed to those who have special needs, and children whose mother tongue is not English as opposed to the vast majority of English speakers. The need to find the most appropriate form of education is driven by the need to enable all children to learn as effectively as possible at school, to identify those pressures which lead to academic failure or social failure for the children, and eliminate them.

As well as the need to find the best form of educational provision, schools also need to develop attitudes and behaviour to support effective learning for all children. Whole school behaviour policies are the vehicles whereby schools can influence the attitudes and behaviour of children towards each other and towards staff, and are specifically concerned with how people behave rather than the ways of organising provision. It is perfectly possible to develop a Special Needs Policy which meets the requirements of the 1993 Education Act on identifying children with special needs and providing for their educational needs but fails to address the issues of how those children are to be included in the school community and the implications of this for the behaviour of others towards them.

A key element in the evolution of whole school behaviour policies, estimating their effectiveness, has been strengthened through the work on anti-bullying policies. Research in a number of places has demonstrated that it is possible to define and measure the incidence of bullying, and that the reductions in the level of bullying following the introduction of a whole school behaviour policy can be measured (Olweus, 1993, Smith and Sharp, 1994, Arora, 1994). This evidence, with the qualitative data from the evaluations of the introduction of the whole school policies, can now be added to the evidence from the studies of the variations between schools conducted by Reynolds and others during the last decade (Reynolds, 1988). This data demonstrates not only that school procedures can make a difference to common performance indicators reflecting various aspects of children's alienation from school, but that the way in which they do so can be described.

## Social rules in school

The reality of school is that a large number of children and a much smaller number of adults are crammed together in a fairly limited space for a limited period of time. The community has given both the children and the adults tasks to achieve, these being learning tasks for the children and caring, controlling, and educational tasks for the adults. At any one time all the various groups of children and adults have a number of assumptions about how they complete these tasks together. The aims, rules and principles of how these groups plan their activities and communicate are partly assumed, partly stated, and often owe a lot to the history of the particular groups involved. As well as rules and principles about how the tasks are to be achieved, these groups also have rules and principles about how the children behave to each other and to the adults, and how the adults behave to each other and to the children. Again, these rules of behaviour are sometimes stated as general principles, but more often are a relatively unconscious part of how people have behaved towards each other previously.

Just because these rules – both conscious and unconscious – are negotiated to help people live and work together, they normally function reasonably well. From time to time however external circumstances change. Interpersonal tensions arise which disturb the usual patterns of how people communicate. Sometimes other new and possibly even unrecognised subgroups form within the school community which then develop their own sets of rules and expectations of acceptable behaviour.

This book is particularly about developing whole school policies to influence some of those interpersonal rules and expectations of what is the proper way to behave. It specifically focusses on information gathered as a result of research into preventing bullying in school, attempts to minimise tensions arising from racial or cultural differences between children and adults in school, and tensions arising through attempts to integrate children with special needs into the school community. A further area which overlaps with these three is the general area of 'positive behaviour policies'. These attempt to take a general view of acceptable behaviour in school and support teaching staff in working out methods of building a better behaved school.

All educationists have thought about school rules from time to time, to say the least; and much work has been done in clarifying school rules and in communicating them to teachers and children. However the ideal set of school rules as promulgated by the staff does not exist in isolation; it exists in a context where there is already a large number of other rules of behaviour for the different groups of children and the different groups of adults. To be effective school rules should not only be consistent with each other, but they have to mesh with all the other expectations of behaviour held by the constituent groups of people in school. To achieve a successful meshing of all these systems of rules, staff and parents have to recognise the existence of all the other sets of rules existing amongst the children and staff. They must work to minimise the number of times when the children in particular suffer from contrary expectations from two different sources. This chapter contains a review of how informal social groups in school come to develop their own rules and the kinds of rules which they develop. The book will go on to describe in detail ways in which whole school approaches can be developed and implemented with involvement from the greatest possible number of people.

## Standards of behaviour amongst children

When adults use the word 'standards' about children's behaviour, what they usually mean is that children are expected to behave in the ways that the adults think they should. 'Good' or 'bad' standards of behaviour tend to be perceived from the position of the person making the judgement. Everyone can say *'I know what standards of behaviour I expect towards me because I know the rules that I need to operate within the various groups that I am a member of'* The teacher can say this; the head teacher can say this; and the 13 year-old black girl in the middle range of ability can also say this. The problem is of course that each of these individuals would need and expect different standards of behaviour towards them from the people around them. Usually their awareness of each other and their different roles in school means that they can work within the general expectations of the people around them and 'rub along' together reasonably well. There will be inconsistencies, each of them will feel that the other tends not to live up to the ideal standards, but the gap is usually not so great as to cause a breakdown of their patterns of communication. All the children and all the adults in the school are of course in this position, all working with their own expectations as to how people should behave towards them, all being slightly disappointed most of the time, and all managing to live together reasonably well in spite of this. The kinds of rules and expectations we are talking about here are essentially the 'normal' rules and expectations, generated and used by people in an almost unconscious fashion, every minute of the day. We are not talking about situations when individuals find that they just cannot communicate any more, when they cannot either understand the rules which other people expect them to behave by, or understand the rules but have not the slightest wish or inclination to observe them. These more serious occasions do occur when external agencies are called in, and the child leaves school through one route or another, to the accompaniment of a certain amount of anguish all round. Adults also sometimes leave after communication becomes impossible, and everyone breathes a sigh of relief.

**Learning to behave**

Accepting this complexity, how do children learn how to behave? Do they bring with them some instinctive methods of learning how to behave? Are they programmed to test the limits of any social group that they join? In general, their skills at learning other people's expectations of them and some rules for their own behaviour is a developmental process, beginning in the pre-school years and continuing into young adulthood and even beyond. The development of children's understanding and skills in social relationships has been studied extensively by psychologists, and a relatively large amount is known (Erwin, 1993). So much is generally appreciated by teachers, but what is often not appreciated is that this developmental process of learning how to get on with others is a general mechanism which the child then applies to any social group which they are in. Sometimes children join existing social groups, for example when they join a new class; sometimes they create social groups round themselves as groups of friends. In the first case they observe what happens in the class – who talks, what the teacher's reaction is, what the other children's reaction is, what do people do and when and with what results. This process of observation, when added to some personal trial and error, enables them to learn what the expectations of behaviour are inside this particular class. They are dependent upon the other people in the class including the teacher – behaving consistently so that the pattern of activity and the rules governing it that the child observes is the same from one day to the next. Children are of course not all equally skilled in doing this some learn the expectations very quickly, and also learn how far they need to meet other people's expectations fairly quickly as well. Others seem to find great difficulty in recognising these interactional rules and behaving consistently with them. In most children this process is unconscious, and children cannot easily say why they do or do not do certain things. However some children, for example children who have been in a number of children's homes or foster homes, will specifically ask when in doubt *'is this allowed here?'*. They know perfectly well that some things which are allowed in one family or home are not allowed in other families or homes and they have learnt that the quickest way of finding out is to ask.

Whether children are constructing a social group round themselves, or joining an informal group of friends which has already formed, they follow much the same procedures. The main difference is that they can choose whether or not they want to be a member of a particular social group of friends. They do need a group of friends though, and would rather change their behaviour, if they can, to fit the needs of a pre-existing group than not have friends at all. If there are no obvious pre-existing groups of friends whom the newcomer can join, then they seek the company of children who have similar interests to themselves. Any child brings with them their past history of seeking and making friends and forming informal groups, and so at first they try to use the same strategies and approaches, to children with similar interests and needs, that have been successful before. At this initial stage of group formation there is often some conflict and tension. The change in group membership unsettles established relationships and the newcomer(s) will test out group boundaries. As a social group does become established round the child, then the patterns of interaction are less dependent on earlier experience in other groups and become more of a function of the particular social group that is being formed. A similar process occurs when a larger group, such as a form or class group, changes membership. Readers who are teachers may well be able to identify clearly the 'settling in' period at the beginning of a new year or the ripples of conflict which often follow the arrival of a new student or a new teacher.

The general point about both these situations though is that children do come into groups seeking contact. They seek to find out what are the expectations of the other people in the group, both children and adults, and they learn the rules from what they observe happening. Sometimes this is consistent with what is proclaimed as a *'school rule'* but if there is a clash between what the school rule says and what children do, the child will learn the rules of what actually happens. We all live in real social situations, not hypothetical ones.

## Positive behaviour policies

From the school's point of view of course it would be very helpful if the expectations and standards of behaviour that were developed amongst the groups of children were relatively consistent with the needs of the educational tasks of the school, with the expectations of other groups of chil-

dren, and with the general set of school rules themselves, i.e. the for-
malised and verbally stated principles as to what is acceptable behaviour.
There is no intrinsic reason why this should not be the case – the psychological purpose of social groups of children and of adults having clear
expectations and rules amongst themselves is that they do make life easier. They help to make the reactions of other people as predictable and
supportive as possible given the tasks which the various groups have to
perform. However, many expectations and rules which are generated
inside groups of children are to do with maintaining the integrity and identity of the members of that group, and maintaining a sense of security and
support from the other members of the group. The same, incidentally, also
applies to the various groups of adults in the school. However, as anyone
who has ever entered a school is all too well aware, the nature of the learning tasks that schools are set to achieve and the particular administrative
conditions in which to achieve them are not necessarily consistent with the
expectations of appropriate behaviour existing in the groups. Just to take a
very simple example, one very common assumption of many learning
tasks at all levels is that they are directed toward writing something down.
In fact for almost all groups of children and adults speech is by far the preferred method of communication and one which most children and adults
use most of the time. It is not particularly surprising then that the element
of writing in learning tasks is one which children constantly try to minimise and in doing so provoke many minor moments of tension between
themselves and the staff.

The efforts to establish *'positive behaviour policies' are* explicit efforts
to encourage school staff, and sometimes some groups of children as well,
to think through and articulate just what are the necessary expectations
that the adults and children in the school should have of each other
(Galvin, Mercer and Costa, 1989). Having clarified expectations and having looked at these expectations with some regard to the necessary learning tasks that the school has to carry out, it then becomes possible to state
them clearly and refer to them in situations where the rules are not being
observed. This increases the sense of security both for the adults and for
the children, and can often lead to a considerable·reduction in the often
minor disagreements and misunderstandings that arise.

## School Rules

This discussion above highlights the complexity of the social world which
the system of school rules attempts to structure and limit in some ways.
The discussion also reveals how difficult it is for a set of school rules to
have a positive impact on children's behaviour unless they recognise some
of the needs of the various groups of children and the informal expectations of appropriate behaviour which those groups give rise to. Rules

which are not meshed into the social reality of the groups of children and groups of staff in school can only be enforced at the price of constant reiteration and sanctions for non-observance, which will inevitably lead to the children becoming increasingly alienated from the adults who are trying to enforce the rules. The whole area of school uniforms gives many examples of this. If the school uniform rules are framed in such a way so as to permit the youngsters to acknowledge some part of current fashion, rather than to specifically reject any possibility of the children relating to the world of dress outside the school, much unnecessary friction can be avoided.

## Developing Whole School Policies on Appropriate Behaviour

To ensure that explicit school rules and expectations are not unnecessarily at odds with the expected behaviour from the other sub-groups comprising the school community, some process of early consultation with those other groups, both of children and of teachers can be a great help. The process of developing a whole school policy about acceptable behaviour involves consultation with all those who will be affected by those rules. The process of consultation ensures that the reasons for the development of the rules have been clearly thought through and accepted as reasonable by those who will have to implement the rules and those who will have to conform to them. In other words the processes of consultation at a time when the rules are being reviewed assists both the understanding of the rules and the acceptance of them by the school community. It also enables monitoring and review processes to be put in place to get some kind of managerial handle on when and how the rules are not being conformed to. Much of this book concerns ways of establishing these whole school policies on different aspects of behaviour which influence the behaviour of children and adults in the school. In the sections following we will briefly sketch out some of the specific group dynamics in three types of situations where tensions and anxieties arise in groups of children and between children and adults, interfering with the smooth flow of everyday school life. These three areas are bullying amongst children in schools, tensions arising from children and staff coming from different ethnic or cultural groups, and the process whereby children with various disabilities are integrated into mainstream school. Tensions involved in this last process are of course quite difficult to perceive unless the emotional adjustment of the children with special needs is very carefully monitored. Most of the negative consequences of inappropriate behaviour in school in this instance falls on the children with disabilities themselves rather than on other members of the school community. For example some of the research into aspects of bullying has demonstrated that children with special needs attending units in mainstream schools are more than twice as likely to suffer bullying and teasing than children of the same age and background are who do not have special needs.

*The Process of Establishing Whole School Behaviour Policies*

This book draws upon knowledge, acquired through school based research, which indicates that the process of achieving a successful social behaviour policy can be clearly defined. This process necessitates the meaningful involvement of all staff and students and clear leadership from senior management. The willing participation of the broader school community is established at the first stage by identifying a need for such a policy. Once it is accepted within the school that such a policy is required, then information about the issue will receive more positive attention. An informed community will be able to engage more thoroughly in discussion and consultation about the issue and are more likely to accept collective responsibility for implementing the policy when it is finally established. Communication, training and monitoring assist with continued implementation of the policy over time. Review procedures enable long term improvement of the policy. In the following chapters, various aspects of this process are examined and discussed.

# CHAPTER 2

# The Dynamics of Victimisation and Rejection in School

## Bullying in school – its origins and incidence

Bullying has been long recognised in the English education system but until very recently has been ignored by researchers. Almost all the research has occurred since 1985, and has been paralleled by increasing concern amongst parents, politicians and schools, often stimulated by some tragic and high profiled instances where school children have been bullied to the end of their tether. The research has typically concentrated on three themes; the characteristics of the children who bully, the characteristics of the children who are bullied, and the bullying process itself – how often does bullying occur, and what measures can be used to prevent it occurring so frequently. During this same period various bodies and institutions have made determined efforts to reduce the amount of bullying that occurs in their school, or in their local education authority. A number of local education authorities have mounted large scale surveys followed by intervention training (Humberside, Wolverhampton), and one of these large scale intervention attempts was mounted by Sheffield University and Sheffield Local Education Authority, supported by a grant from the Department for Education. This survey and intervention study involved 23 schools in Sheffield, two thirds primary and one third secondary, and many of the matters discussed in this book relate to that study. Particular outcomes from the study include detailed training materials and procedures for reducing bullying in schools which are found to be successful and these will be available nationally. One of the earlier findings of that study was that many schools in fact already had whole school policies in existence, concerned with special needs, or positive behaviour. A key question for these schools in devising and structuring their policies was to decide the best ways to blend their initiatives in several of these fields together, to give a more cohesive and more all-embracing overall policy.

## The Effects of Bullying and Harassment on Student Well-being and Learning

Few, if any, children actually enjoy being bullied or harassed. It tends to make their lives in school, and even out of school, miserable. Olweus (1993) demonstrates that persistently bullied boys have lower self-esteem than other boys. Sharp (1994) investigated how stressful secondary aged pupils found bullying and how they coped with this. Of a sample of 723 students, 40 per cent had experienced bullying in some form over the previous school year. Between one third and three quarters of these pupils found bullying behaviour highly stressful. Having nasty stories or rumours spread was reported as most stressful, with name calling (including racist name calling), social exclusion and being physically attacked or verbally threatened also being rated as very unpleasant or upsetting. One in ten students reported that the bullying behaviour had affected their health – making them feel ill or experience difficulty with sleeping. A third felt very panicky or nervous and a similar number complained of impaired concentration in school. Twelve per cent would often take time off school to avoid being bullied; 14 per cent would respond aggressively to the bullying and a disturbing 9 per cent would actually hurt themselves in an attempt to cope with their feelings.

These kinds of statistics demonstrate to us that we cannot be complacent about bullying and harassment, or indeed any kind of discrimination. These kinds of destructive behaviours can inhibit the learning potential of young people in our schools. It can affect their health, their achievement and their attendance. It is therefore of great importance for schools to counter these problems through the development of effective behaviour policies.

## Characteristics of Children who are Bullied and who Bully Others

Many of the characteristics of both these groups have been effectively described by Besag (1989) and Olweus (1993). In outline, children who are bullied tend to be relatively ineffective at making social links with their age mates and lack confidence in physical skills.

Children who bully on the other hand, tend to be active and assertive, not to mention aggressive, and also tend to see aggression as a perfectly acceptable way of getting their own way in a group. They are also more likely to come from both families and sub-cultures where aggression is seen as an acceptable way of conducting social relationships. Rather surprisingly, they are not particularly unpopular with their own peer group, if socio-metric studies are to be believed, but this may be because the bullying process itself involves some formation and maintenance of support for the bully from a particular group of friends. The apparent only slightly less than average popularity of children who bully may indicate only that the peer group are very divided in their response to the children who bully, some of whom would gain support and contact with a particular section of the peer group but avoidance and rejection from another section. Additionally, there may be some overlap or confusion between 'social power' and 'popularity' – those who possess social power may be seen as desirable companions for that reason alone.

## The Bullying Process

Looking at research data on the personalities of both groups of children, and at other observation and interview data, it is possible to describe the bullying process. Much literature on bullying describes a strong social element – the bully is very frequently accompanied by a group of friends or even a wider group of acolytes and the victim is either not at all related to this group, or is very much a loner on the fringes trying to gain access into the group. There is rarely any material gain from the bullying for the children who bully and their friends. Victims tend to define bullying as *'being picked on for no reason'* (Arora and Thompson, 1987). From the point of view of many such children, the experience of being bullied comes out of the blue as a random event that has no relationship whatsoever to their normal emotional life. This is not always the case; there are persistent descriptions in the literature (Olweus, 1978, 1993 and Besag, 1989) of a small group of victims, possibly around 10 to 15 per cent, who can be called. 'provocative victims' in that they may have a tendency to make persistently mirror aggressive responses to the bully or their group. These children are attempting to establish or maintain some kind of relationship with the bully and their social group, in this instance involving much semi-ritualised aggressive behaviour.

In the majority of cases, the one who gains out of the bullying is very definitely the children doing the bullying. What is it that they do gain? A very important clue comes from asking adolescents why do bullies behave like that. A very common response is *'to show off to his mates'* (Thompson and Arora, 1991 and Keise, 1992). Someone showing off to their mates by dominating and causing pain to an innocent bystander is demonstrating to their group their capacity for dominance using aggression, and maintaining their own position as leader in that group in doing so. To demonstrate that capacity for aggression inside the friendship group would be likely to damage the cohesion of that group, and so an outsider is chosen. In particular the children looking for a victim would look for a child, ideally alone, who could be easily dominated using aggressive means, thus minimising the possibility that the process of domination would not work.

One very disturbing feature of bullying is the length of time that established patterns continue to occur. Again, from the point of view of the bullying child it is equally effective to demonstrate this capacity to use aggression on the same victim as it would be with different victims, and in addition once a victim has experienced the role it is likely that achieving the necessary damnation would be easier on subsequent occasions. In consequence, patterns of the same child acting as a bully and another particular child being bullied can continue over quite long periods of time, commonly for years (Cole, 1977 and Olweus, 1979, 1993). In this way the interaction between the children involved in bullying is to a certain extent ritualised and predictable and once one child has established obvious dominance over another the specific incident can cease. All involved understand this, and they also understand that normally the level of aggression is very carefully controlled, to the minimum necessary to establish and maintain a totally dominant position, with minimum effort. In fact, the relatively controlled and ritualised nature of bullying is very much in the interest of the victim, as well as the bully, because it decreases the possibility that less controlled violence may occur. A point clarified by Olweus (1993), following some discussion work, is to challenge the notion held by some teachers that children who bully are in some way lacking in self-esteem. He demonstrates clearly that they are not, and that the problem is more to teach them to maintain their self-image for activities which do not involve the automatic use of aggression and violence.

## Bullying Amongst Girls

Early research on the differences between bullying amongst boys and amongst girls seem to indicate that girls were appreciably less likely to be involved either as bullies or as victims than boys (Besag, 1989). The process does seem to reflect a different mix of influences amongst girls than amongst boys, and bullying amongst girls seems to be more associated with social exclusion and alienation from friendship groups (Keise, 1992). Similarly, some theories of bullying amongst girls suggests that the motivation for girls to bully may be directly related to strengthening the affiliation with a group of friends by demonstrating the exclusion of another. This may well be the case, but it is still related to the same basic mechanism of group membership and their status and involvement in that group for the bully. More recent work on the incidence of bullying seems to suggest that the incidence of bullying amongst boys and girls is not as different as the early research suggested. The apparent differences in some situations may be related more to the difficulty of clear definition of bullying when the processes are much more psychological than physical and more closely related to the 'normal' dynamics of friendship and rejection amongst children. From the instance of developing whole school policies however, it is fairly clear that any policy should involve boys and girls equally, and should be couched in terms which both boys and girls can easily relate to. Keise (op.cit.) provides very interesting data on bullying in single sex schools (boys and girls), generally supporting the dynamics of bullying reported above. Additionally, she stresses that for some girls, using aggression in the course of daily interaction is a way of rejecting one of the cultural stereotypes of girls as being weak, dependent on boys' protection, and unable to assert themselves effectively. She also gives a good discussion of the overlap between bullying and racism, in particular the power of bullying using racist name-calling, and how the black children can seek to gain acceptance by a white majority by joining in the bullying of more isolated black children. She also raises the issue of sexism in schools, as being heavily implicated in the group dynamics of rejection.

## How Much Bullying Actually Goes On?

This has been one of the central questions of virtually all the research done to date, and some general conclusions can be drawn. A rough guide would be that at least 10 per cent of children in our schools are probably involved in bullying at any one time, either as a bully or a victim. Many figures from particular schools or particular settings are considerably higher than this, especially if varied definitions of bullying are used, or if different sets of informants are used. Reports from parents indicate that roughly one quarter of parents have come across the problem with their own children. Using a behavioural definition of bullying arrived at by the children themselves, Arora and Thompson (1987) showed that between 10 per cent and roughly 40 per cent of children had experienced aggressive incidents of a type which they would call bullying more than once in the week previous to the survey. Olweus (1985a) working in Scandinavia, gave general average figures of 5 per cent of children seriously involved in bullying and 15 per cent occasionally involved. Of these roughly 10 per cent were classified as victims and 8 per cent as bullies. One common 'finding' is that whenever schools do either their own surveys or participate in surveys run by groups of researchers, the outcome is that there is a lot more bullying happening in their school than they would have anticipated. For certain more specialised groups, for example children with statements of special needs being educated in integrated settings, research results indicate that the incidence of bullying can be much higher, with roughly half or more of the sample saying that they had been the victims of bullying (Thompson, Whitney and Smith, in press). The incidence of bullying reported in primary schools seems to be greater than that reported in secondary schools, although intervention programmes seem to find it easier to reduce bullying in primary schools than in secondary schools. Whole school policies and other preventative programmes seem to need to be in operation for appreciably longer in secondary schools to take effect than they do in primary schools (Arora, in press).

16

*Assessment of the Incidence of Bullying for Monitoring Effectiveness of Whole School Policies*

There are various ways that this can be done, many of them quite quick and simple, involving child surveys, teacher surveys, or cumulative recording of incidents with certain characteristics. Estimation of the incidents can either be planned and executed completely by the school (following the guidelines given in more detail later); or if necessary the school can involve outside agencies to help them plan the data gathering and even, if they wish to, carry out the data gathering for the school. In general however, we would strongly recommend that the staff and pupils collect the data and are involved in the analysing of it. Staff need to be very clear about the reasons why the policies are operating and what the expected benefit from them will be. Involvement in the analysis of monitoring data is a very important way of becoming aware, and can help to motivate staff to implement the policies and to look for changes in incidence over time. One way in which outside agencies can help schools is to support their initial attempts to show incidence surveys through provision of instruments, possibly with some comparative data on variation in incidence between schools. Research projects in particular can be well placed to support schools in this way (Smith and Sharp, 1994 and Olweus, 1993).

**Tensions in multi-cultural and multi-racial schools**

We talked a little in the last section about how the groups and the subgroups to which people felt they 'belong' to various degrees influenced the standards of behaviour which they conformed to. One kind of subgroup is that of 'ethnic background'. The term 'ethnic background' is here taken to mean that the person concerned – the children or the adult – are members of ethnic groups who see themselves as culturally distinct from other ethnic groups in a society, and are recognised by members of other groups as being distinct. The usual characteristics which lead to ethnic groups seeing themselves as different are their recent history, their language, their styles of dress, and their religion. Skin colour may also be relevant, but this is very difficult to generalise on, as some ethnic groups contain individuals with widely different skin colours. In the U.K. some authors (Dickinson, 1982 and Swan, 1985) see those people of Irish descent as being from one of the largest ethnic minorities, and other long established groups are those from Italian backgrounds, Jewish backgrounds, and Chinese backgrounds. Frequently the term ethnic group is used to refer to groups who are distinct from the 'white (European)' majority – i.e. in addition to the cultural differences referred to above, their skin is darker to some degree. Even this situation is further complicated as soon as it is examined – for instance a large number of the individuals who would see themselves as members of the black community are in fact part of a 'Black (British)' community – speaking with broad midlands, home counties, or northern accents, and taking part in the usual aspects of 'British' culture as their white counterparts of a similar age are doing.

All the activities, attitudes and behaviour, which go to make up membership of an ethnic minority in the U.K. are wholly learned, with the sole exception of skin colour. In very remote regions of the world a certain amount of natural selection may have taken place to encourage other major physical features (for example height or body build), but by the time individuals from those families have moved, settled and found themselves relating to a particular ethnic group in Britain, sufficient genetic mixing has usually occurred to minimise the significance of these other physical features. In addition the genetic make up of the U.K. population is very varied with respect to these other physical features, and so the features themselves do not give any distinct difference from all the other ethnic groups in the U.K.

## Group standards and individual identity

Everyone needs to make relationships with a particular group of people (or usually more than one group) with whom they share experiences, lifestyles, and also ways of interpreting the world around them. The groups also make some contributions towards the sense of identity of the individual concerned. This sense of identity, this sense of self, is not something which we mature into as we grow older. It is something which is given to us from the people with whom we interact. Other people idolise us, accept us, neglect us, or reject us. We learn that they see us as being good at some things and bad at others, and we collect a range of attributes which are largely defined by people in the various groups we come into contact with. If we are accepted by the members of a group, then we see ourselves as members of that group, we share meanings with other people in that group, and we in general tend to accept the standards of behaviour seen as the norm by the other people in that group. This process of gaining identity from different social groups is usually expressed through the means of dress, non-verbal communicative behaviour, and language. These identity forming processes are occurring around us all the time, and most readers will be quite familiar with them. There are however three crucial implications of them which are sometimes less widely recognised than they should be.

The first of these is that these processes of group formation and identity formation are central to the development and everyday life of all of us. Sometimes their affects may be deplored if they appear to lead to conflict between groups, but the processes themselves are crucial and cannot be denied.

The second implication is that every individual belongs to a number of overlapping social groups. Any school child is a member of their family, their neighbourhood peer group, their school, their year group, their class, and a particular friendship group inside the class. They are also members of a gender group – boys or girls – and receive many influences from that (Duveen and Lloyd, 1993). They may well be a member of more than one friendship group inside the class, each with differing standards and expectations of behaviour. Accordingly, their sense of identity also comes from the full range of groups that they are members of. To behave towards any individual as though they are only a member of one group is at best a gross over-simplification, and at worst behaviour which leads the child to perceive themselves as being unreasonably rejected by the other, as the other's behaviour appears to deny relationships which the child knows exist.

The third implication is that as we are all members of our particular set of groups, we explicitly do not share meanings with those who are members of other groups at the same level in the group hierarchy described above. For example if two individuals are members of the general group labelled 'school teaching staff' but one is a female member of that group and another a male member, then there will be some meanings which will not be shared by the other. The same applies to male and female groups of children, to groups of children of different ages, and of course to groups of children from different ethnic backgrounds. The problem is of course that no-one has any way of knowing what are the meanings that are held by members of other groups but not by their own. This knowledge is not impossible to acquire – it depends on some detailed communications with some members of the other group – but our understanding of the meanings held by individuals from other groups is limited by our lack of experience. Lacking knowledge of these other meanings, we then tend to react as though these other meanings did not exist, and thereby tend to portray ourselves as relatively ignorant, insensitive, and rejecting of individuals who do belong to other groups. These reactions lead to the strengthening of the perceived differences between the groups, producing a mild mutual rejection at the boundaries. Conversely, when we show some understanding of the existence and nature of different sets of meanings to our own when communicating with members of a different group, even if we do not actually share those meanings ourselves, then this process of mild rejection does not occur. The problems with mild rejection is that it can very easily extend, through repeated incidents of a similar nature, to more and more intense rejection, leading to situations where members of the opposing groups find it extremely difficult to communicate with each other at all, even on mutual and 'objective' information.

As can be seen from the above discussions, all these processes are in fact perfectly 'natural' processes, arising from the need of us all to find supportive social groups and establish a sense of identity and self confidence which permits us to act positively in the world. The tensions related to being members of different ethnic groups are no different in kind to the tensions associated with difference in age inside the same ethnic group. However tensions between members of different ethnic groups can rise to extremely important levels in schools, so one of the applications of the development of whole school policies to be considered later in the book are concerned with whole school policies on race and cultural identity.

*Specific Difficulties Arising in Schools*

After considering the processes of group membership and individual identity above, we can then go on to recognise the specific points at which tensions emerge in schools either between children of different ethnic backgrounds or between staff and children of different ethnic backgrounds. These can be summarised from the above discussion as:

1. Where the adult reacts to the child in a way which drastically over-simplifies their group membership system, typically by assuming that the fact that the child comes from one (assumed homogenous) kind of ethnic minority group implies that certain behaviour can always be expected of them.
2. To behave in a way which implies that actions by the child are determined by their being a member of a given ethnic group, and are not a matter of individual choice by the child themselves.

Examples of both types of incorrect assumptions are described in detail in Gillborn (1990). Through detailed observation and informal interviewing he establishes, for example, that the teachers in the school studied tended to assume that because some particular individual boys had ethnic backgrounds from the Asian sub-continent, they would be much more likely to accept 'school related' values of academic achievement, and persistence in tasks to fulfil that, than was justified by the boys' actual reaction itself. Likewise in the same school some of the adults reacted consistently incorrectly by assuming that because some boys again were seen to be members of the Afro-Caribbean sub-culture that their values were particularly 'anti-school', and more specifically, were rejecting of a general ethos of school attainment and were likely to be motivated by an explicit wish to challenge the authority of the teachers. This led the teachers to impose sanctions of various kinds on children (usually boys) from the Afro-Caribbean ethnic backgrounds on the basis of the teacher's interpretation of the likelihood of future events rather than on the basis of any events which had actually occurred. Not surprisingly, these particular actions were highly resented by the children concerned and seen as specifically rejecting of both the children themselves and of the community involved.

The same study detailed how children's groups were usually based on commonalities other than ethnic background. For example, children from Afro-Caribbean backgrounds were not only associating and forming groups with other children from the same backgrounds, and most of the children's groups were actually drawn from children of different ethnic origins – some white, some Indian, and some Afro-Caribbean. The groups did change with time as some individuals gradually moved out of the group and other individuals moved in. Friendship groups based on activities or popularity were more common than those based on sharing ethnic backgrounds. The behaviour of particular individuals could only be understood and predicted from the basis of knowing those particular individuals in some detail, not from predicting their behaviour by their presumed 'membership' of a particular defined ethnic minority group.

**Tensions between groups of children from different backgrounds**

Children can form groups exclusively defined by a shared cultured background under certain circumstances. There tends to be two sets of circumstances where this happens, the first as the combination of the distancing process described above, whereby members of different ethnic groups understand so little of the meanings and standards of other groups that the non-communication between them is felt as rejection and hostility based on membership of that particular ethnic group. This spiral of behaviour is of course self-perpetuating – the less communication occurs, the more rejection is perceived, and the less communication again occurs. The second main reason why children turn to groups of their own ethnic background is security. Whenever there is a persistent but normally low level of aggression in schools (or anywhere else for that matter), individuals seek security from their perceived source of threat. For example in a recent study where children were asked *'what is the best way for you to prevent yourself being bullied?'* the universal answer from 14 year old boys was *'you go around with your mates'* (Thompson and Arora, 1991). If the aggression experienced is specifically related to colour or ethnic background, then the natural group of mates to turn to for protection is those of the same ethnic background or colour as yourself, those equally implicated in the aggressive stand-off. The support group does not have to be racially defined in this way, but if it is not to be defined in this way the children concerned need to have had plenty of opportunity to develop strong peer group relationships with children with different ethnic backgrounds. This does happen naturally, and can be specifically facilitated by action taken in school. The likelihood of being able to develop friendship groups and support groups including children of different ethnic backgrounds clearly partly depends on the proportion of children from the various different backgrounds attending the same school. As a proportion of children from the specifically ethnic minority backgrounds increases in school, the more likely it is purely from a statistical basis that children in friendship groups and support groups will include more and more children from that background.

Under certain conditions tensions are likely to develop either between adults and children of different ethnic backgrounds, or between children from different ethnic backgrounds. In both of these instances the sharing of support and common meanings between people from the same background gradually increases to a shared common identity, to give support for the particular individuals who feel themselves rejected by those from different backgrounds. This strengthening of ethnically-based identity also makes the probability of tensions between people from the different ethnic backgrounds more likely, as membership of the same ethnic background becomes more and more necessary and common as a defining characteristic of those friendship groups which provide a supportive and protective social world. When a certain point is reached, the key question becomes not how individuals perceive themselves as members of differing groups, but how groups defined by different ethnic backgrounds can negotiate with each other to achieve more or less stable spheres of influence with as little damage as possible. It is unlikely that many schools in the UK will be facing situations of this type, but when it does occur tensions are very high and very difficult to deal with by the staff.

## Tensions between children as being reflections of tensions in the community

One of the contributing factors towards tensions in school occurs when the initial threat, and consequential reference group definition based on ethnic background, has already occurred before the children come on to the school grounds. Most children wish to relate to as wide a range of people as possible around them, and in their earlier years see activity and popularity as much more interesting reasons for group formation than meeting perceived threats. However if the adults in a given ethnic minority community feel themselves under threat, they are very likely to pass this awareness on to their children, and encourage their children to find safety by associating with friends from the same background. In this they are often encouraged by the religious leaders of their communities, who would see their specific religious mission as encouraging uniformity of religious belief and practise, and for this reason would encourage their youngsters to associate primarily with others from their own community. These processes again occur in all cultures and all shades of religious belief, and the trick which most people are trying to learn is how to find a way which maintains a strong sense of identity and security through support mechanisms based in family culture whilst at the same time enabling the youngsters to be open enough to communicate effectively with members of other communities, in order to achieve economic success and a general social stability. Such issues of identity and security may feel much more relevant for members of an ethnic minority who do not feel they have much power in their general social situation, and find it difficult to trust the general social mechanisms of public institutions to give them protection and justice. All this may seem a long way from developing positive behaviour policies in school, but as some children come to school from these backgrounds, policies and practices which fail to recognise the extent of the tensions felt in school will probably meet only partial success.

## Tensions arising from integration of children with special needs into mainstream schools

Children with special needs have always formed a part of the school community. Most schools have a long history of making some kinds of special arrangements to deliver effective education to children with special needs, usually by having a small group of staff who are particularly concerned for their educational and emotional development. The extent and sophistication of such arrangements have increased over the years. This is especially true in secondary schools where the much larger number of teachers coming into contact with any one child and the much larger number of children in the school have meant that specific administrative and educational arrangements have been made. Typically these have taken the form of a special needs department, operating on a combination of withdrawal and in-class support basis; and a pastoral care support system. These extra services are nominally for all children in school, but in practice staff spend much more time with those children experiencing some kind of difficulties; and they are often headed by one of the deputy heads of the school. During the 1980s awareness has gradually increased of the nature of needs which were 'special' beginning with the now notorious estimate by the Warnock Committee that from 16 to 18 per cent of children of school age could be considered to have some special needs at some time during their school career. This was rapidly followed by the 1981 Education Act paying considerable attention to institutionalising best practice with regard to the assessment of children's needs and the process whereby provision was made for them. The 1981 Act also brought in the possibility that at some point legislation might state a preference for education in mainstream schools rather than education in special schools wherever that was possible. More and more commonly, schools had 'units' or 'special resources' as a part of the school structure. With the 1988 Act and the 1993 Act the responsibilities of schools specifically to identify and meet the needs of children became more specific still, and the 1993 Act in particular made it a duty of the Governors that they should use their best endeavours to ensure that all registered pupils who had special needs were identified by the school staff, that their needs were communicated to all staff who might teach them, and that their needs should be met in school.

## Difficulties in meeting usual school expectations

The usual points in the school system where difficulties are experienced occur when the children who have special needs seem to be unable to meet the general expectations of the school for both academic learning and some aspects of behaviour. Making such generalisations is very risky, because doing so masks the huge variation amongst children with special needs in the nature of the precise difficulty which they have, but in general it is fairly true to say that most arrangements in school are planned and delivered on the basis of an educational system which meets the needs of 80 per cent of children in it. By definition, children who have 'special' needs are distinctively different from the majority of children in school (Education Act 1993). The pressure points typically come then where the usual arrangements made in school to encourage children to learn and behave appropriately do not work for children with special needs. The first response of the system of course is to repeat its expectations more loudly and clearly, but when repeated failure occurs it is clear to everyone involved that something more than this is needed. In some way the 'normal' expectations have to be made more flexible, and acceptable alternative expectations and standards have to be decided on and communicated to staff. Typically the special needs system and the pastoral care system and the staff involved have to be able to communicate information about the nature of the amended arrangements required by children with special needs to other teachers in the school. Indeed, they have to communicate the same information to the other children in the school. Those people most centrally involved of course are the children with special needs themselves and those teachers who are concerned for their progress and welfare. The tensions occur because the children may not learn as efficiently as their classmates; they may misunderstand instructions and find it difficult to understand the tasks being set in class. They will almost certainly feel a range of heightened emotions resulting in part from these failures, and appear as children who maybe anxious, maybe very shy, and maybe isolated from their peers. They may find it difficult to communicate with teachers or indeed any adults, may find it difficult to ask for help in class, may find it difficult to complete work on time, and on occasions may behave quite inappropriately with children or with the teachers in the school. Teachers may find it difficult to predict their behaviour, they may behave appreciably more aggressively than is required, they may find it difficult to attend to work for more than a few minutes, and are fairly commonly unable to give any reasonable explanation for why they behave like this. The tensions are felt as failure by the children, as unwanted aggression and as failure by the teaching staff, who see their best efforts leaking away through the sands of a hundred minor frictions.

The psychological basis for many of these tensions is that the children with special needs are unable to meet some or possibly even many of the normal expectations of the school as a community and the 'official' groups within that such as their subject teaching lessons, tutor groups. the sports teams. The children also find it difficult to meet the expectations of most of the informal friendship groups of their age in school, and their social contacts are likely to be more limited in extent and influence. They may be more vulnerable to exploitation by some children in school; they are certainly more vulnerable to becoming victims of bullying. They tend to feel excluded from the groups recognised as meeting the academic targets in school, and they may well be specifically included in groups which are obviously composed of those who are not achieving academic targets the 'dumbos' and the 'thickies'. They may often come to rely on social contacts with other children with special needs, at the same time recognising all the other children in school with whom they would like to be friends with but do not know how. These relative failures lead to anxiety, feeling rejected by the group, and becoming further alienated from attempting to achieve academic targets which is so obviously so difficult.

In practice of course, teachers everywhere do try to alleviate as many of these problems as they can in the course of their everyday teaching duties, and the school itself responds to their needs through its special needs and pastoral care systems. Need for a whole school policy arises because special needs children form a considerable minority of the school, they are scattered randomly across the school, and they come into contact with a very large proportion of the teaching staff for different purposes. If their time in school is to be supportive and an effective learning experience across the full width of the curriculum, most of both staff and children will need to know how to behave towards them, precisely because the 'normal' expectations of behaviour may well not be fulfilled.

In practice, in the corridors and classrooms in schools, social life is much more varied than is portrayed here. Children who do have quite distinct special needs may only have those needs in one area of life, and can integrate effectively into friendship groups and work groups focussed around other activities. The so-called 'normal' four-fifths of the school population are nothing like as homogeneous as might be thought from these descriptions so far. They contain a large number of assorted groups of children, and the chances of any individual child with special needs being able to make links with at least a few of them are quite high. In one way this diversity in detail of both the special needs children and the others is helpful in that it maximises the opportunities for them to interact with and learn from other children in activities approved by school. On the other hand it makes it appreciably harder for the school staff to know when they should react to any individual child as a 'special' child, and when they should react to them as though they are a perfectly normal member of any particular group. The whole school policy helps them make appropriate judgements on their feet.

**The contributions of whole school policies in these areas**

A large number of the people in school – certainly a great majority of staff and hopefully most of the children – need to hold similar expectations about what is appropriate behaviour when encountering potentially destructive processes caused by stereotyping and exclusion. The school as a whole creates one of those social groups in which children live and learn, and many expectations and standards of behaviour can be identified for the children and taught through the activities of the staff and those silent majority of children who form the bulk of the school community. These standards of behaviour are partly actively taught by schools, acting as agents of socialisation for the community, and partly they are identified and maintained by the school as a reflection of those standards expected by the community outside the school gate. To achieve effective description and communication of these standards expected to the children across the whole school, management does need to make a specific effort. In the next chapter we will look at some of the psychological processes behind effective management of whole school policy implementation.

CHAPTER 3

# The Management of Whole School Behaviour Policies

## Whole school policies as a response to need for systematic development

Management tasks are sometimes divided into maintenance functions and development functions. One of the elements of the maintenance functions is to ensure that the existing school systems are continuing to function in the face of the inevitable minor buffetings from relatively small scale random events. From time to time, it is possible to identify regularities emerging in these sequence of small scale events which means that there is some larger pressure behind them which needs tackling specifically. The need for specific whole school policies very often emerges in this fashion, when many of these minor buffetings are seen to be related together and to represent processes in the organisation which need to be directly addressed by the management team. Some necessary developments of this kind can be addressed by the management team alone. If a set of events constantly poses problems because they do not happen to be part of anyone's formal or informal job description, then one possible response of the management team is to redefine or re-negotiate someone's job description.

However, for issues which essentially concern all the people in the school, then such specific action by a management team alone to 'solve' the general problem emerging is woefully inadequate. Certainly for the issues considered here, (bullying, relations between people from different ethnic groups, and the effective incorporation of children with special needs into the school community) all members of the school – pupils, teaching staff, and all other staff, have to be involved in the implementation of any policy. The school community has to achieve effective definition of policy in a way which can be related to the social positions of everyone in the school, and to achieve effective understanding and commitment to the operation of the policy. To succeed, the whole school has to be involved in the full range of processes of identification of the need for a policy, working out what that policy might be, implementing it, and monitoring its effectiveness. It follows then that whole school policies are most easily attained in those areas of concern that can be most easily described, and where most of the school community would like all members of the school to act in a co-ordinated way. The most obvious example of this is in fact bullying – in almost all schools all the school community (except perhaps the bullies themselves) know bullying occurs, do not like what they know, and can readily accept and approve involvement in a whole school policy to minimise it. In the two other areas considered here, relations between ethnic groups and the inclusion of children with special needs, such favourable attitudes would not be held as generally by most of the school community. Typically, appreciably more of the staff and the children would be relatively neutral towards the establishment of such a policy, seeing the issues as essentially not concerning them. In these areas, the initial leadership exercised by the management team has to be more energetic and specific in disseminating and identifying the need for the policy and the ways in which the lack of such a policy is disadvantageous to the school. The subsequent development of the whole school policies then becomes a part of the organisational development tasks of management, and needs to be linked into the general aims of the school as understood by management.

### Values Behind Whole School Policies and Implications for Management

It will become clearer by now that because whole school policies are designed to describe, to rally general support for, and to implement general standards of behaviour across the school, we are close to talking about something that is commonly known as 'values'. Values can be described as commonly held beliefs as to what actions are important, and demonstrating this by giving attention to what is important by various means spending time on these activities, giving social rewards to people who support these activities and making public statements as to the importance of the activities. The word 'values' itself seems to belong to that vague ethical and religious part of our general culture, and would not be a word that many pragmatic educationists would use too often. However, because school managers are inevitably involved in school leadership, and because in some situations leadership involves identifying and publicising the common principles which lie behind educational activities, it is worthwhile spending a little time here thinking about the implications of values for implementation of a whole school policy.

The psychological roots of values, in common with shared assumptions about what is appropriate behaviour, lie in the phrase 'commonly held beliefs'. Commonly held by whom? What is the group to which the values belong? Values no less than expectations about standards of behaviour, do not exist in a limbo somewhere above our heads. They are an expression of the shared expectations of members of a given group. The apparently esoteric nature of the word 'values' as it is commonly used arises because the group to which it refers is hardly ever specified, except under some global phrase such as 'Western values' or 'Christian values'. Values at this degree of generality may play some part in the general social consciousness of the staff of educational institutions, and give some clues as to the nature of the community the school is educating the children for, but they have precious little meaning for the children except possibly through the principles underlying the criminal justice system and as being reflected in some small sample of their parents' views and opinions. Values only really take on significant meaning for individuals when they are the values reflected in the practice of some particular groups of which they are a member.

Conversely, as we read in chapter 2, groups are partially defined by views and activities held in common. Even for those of us totally unconscious of values, the groups that we belong to will have their assumptions about what is important for group members. These are partly historical, in the sense that they existed in the group before we became a member of it, and partly encouraged and created by the expressed opinions and behaviour of our colleagues in the group. There will tend to be a range of emphasis on any particular issue across members of the group, but in general the great majority of group members would agree to certain value statements which reflect the priorities underlying the group's existence. For example, most adults associated with schools would support the beliefs that schools are basically institutions designed to be as helpful as possible to the children, by teaching them as much of what they need to know as possible before they become adults. Members of school staff would also support the view that they have some responsibility of teaching children how to behave although some would hold this belief more strongly than others. Good behaviour in school is seen as a 'good thing'. Most staff would again subscribe to the value of academic achievements being valued, and possibly to the belief that where possible all children should take examination courses and leave school with certificates attesting to the levels of knowledge they have achieved.

*Testing 'Shared Values'*

Many groups prefer not to ask themselves too many questions about what values they actually hold in common, even though the assumption that they do hold these values underpins group membership. It is usually enough to assume that personal values are shared by others. To actually ask the other members of the group how far they do share these values risks threatening the unity of the group – it is easy to find that the others do not share personal values to the extent to which it had been assumed. Neither do we go around proclaiming values – the group's activities tend to continue until group members support them less and less, when suggestions are made for change. When they are expressed, personal values tend to be expressed in informal off-the-cuff remarks, which are not really intended to investigate or challenge the values held by others, but to wave a particular value as a symbol of group identity.

In a school however the situation is quite different. Schools are agencies operating in *loco parentis* with now statutory duties to teach children not only academic and practical skills but also social attitudes as well. Children are legally obliged to attend school so that the school can discharge these duties. Fine in theory, but the practice is somewhat different. Schools are a collection of social groups of adults and of children, and society's values are often relatively peripheral to the core activities and expectations of these groups. Part of the leadership of the school is to help children rediscover for themselves the central relevance of the core values of the wider community, and to help them learn how to act and to understand their actions in a way which confirms those values. Almost the core central value of society at large is the one restricting violence and threat between its members, and leadership in whole school behaviour policies means identifying and substantiating the need for accepting these particular beliefs and behaving in a way which gives meaning to them.

In teaching community values of this type, the activities consistent with the values, and the statement of values themselves, need to be delivered as separate events. No teacher would assume that being able to state the principle of accepted behaviour is sufficient without matching actions, and many children will behave in a way consistent with those principles but would not be able to say why they are doing so, or what their principles are. Some children (and some adults) will of course be able to state the principles and behave according to them under certain social conditions, but will vary their behaviour when they perceive that the social conditions have changed, and that in this context they can *'get away with it'*. There is no quick way over this conundrum. Large numbers of us will behave in ways which suits our own best interests if we are not part of a group which disapproves of such activity, particularly if we think the risk of being noticed is minimal. In general, if the wider community wishes its members to abide by the general *'Christian values'*, the institutions making up that wider community have to identify and promote those values, both through their rhetoric and through their various practices.

This process of identifying values and the practices which express them occurs during the discussions and consultations involved in setting up the whole school policies. Orthodox research processes have told us that given the choice, the great majority of children and adults would wish to reject bullying and aggression in school (Rigby and Slee, 1993), and the working out of the whole school policy can give them the means to achieve it. The process does need real leadership though and explicit and real commitment to the underlying set of values themselves.

## Managing Public Relations

Almost the first question most managers think of when considering whether to introduce whole school behaviour policies of any kind is '*but what will people think?*'. '*If we launch an anti-bullying policy, are we going to confirm that impression of parents that there is bullying in our school.*' '*How will this affect our public image in the area?*' The same issues potentially would apply to the other special themes as well – if we launch an anti-racist policy, or anti-sexist, does this mean that racism or sexism is rife in school? If we raise the profile of our special needs policy with whole school behaviour elements to it, will people think that our school has a lot of pupils with special needs and that they are being discriminated against? There are some individuals who still have the view that no-one does anything new unless there is a problem to solve. The expectation may have some credibility when considering static adult-based institutions in an unchanging environment, but educational policy and practice has been changing so rapidly over the past twenty years that to expect that things only change when there is a problem is naive in the extreme. The presence of such people does mean however that the presentation of whole school policy development does need to be thought through, to ensure that the benefits from the whole school policy in the eyes of the public very clearly outweigh any possible disadvantages.

One of the keys to effective public presentation of the work towards establishing a policy is clearly then to root this particular initiative in its managerial context. At present this context is that most schools are committed to continuous reviews of procedures and practices, including reviews of their general behaviour policies. The specific issue of bullying having received somewhat of a high profile in the last few years, and evaluation of best practice has demonstrated further ways in which schools may want to adapt and focus their existing policies. Additionally, there has been a comparatively large amount of research in this area recently, all indicating that bullying is more common than was previously thought, and also indicating that appropriate policies can significantly reduce it. Another general theme of course is that with the introduction of the OFSTED inspection system, in future schools will be asked to demonstrate their whole school behaviour policies in this area as a matter of course when an inspection occurs. Given this context, it would be a fairly unimaginative and conservative leadership that would not expect to extend their positive behaviour policies specifically into the bullying area, and then possibly onwards into policies that stress behaviour issues in multi-cultural contexts and in inclusive education contexts.

A further support for taking specific managerial action is the increased public perception of the prevalence of aggression in schools, particularly that based around bullying. Parents are concerned for their children, they pick up and magnify problems reported on local grapevines, and they see stories in the press and on television which only serve to encourage those fears. It would be a brave management team indeed that took a stance that *'there is no bullying here'*, without having considerable evidence to substantiate this. Otherwise, their public would simply not believe them.

One of the main audiences for public relations activities is the parents. To a lesser extent it can also be those children leaving primary school who are about to enter secondary schools, as this is the changeover point at which much parental concern is expressed. This communicates itself to the children, and again reinforces their worries picked up on the primary school grapevines. The main strength of a public relations presentation is clearly to present accurate information, and to do this in a way which demonstrates that it is not merely rhetoric. Parents need to have opportunities to meet with members of staff, and to discuss their concerns with those staff, before their child enters school. In the same way the entrance arrangements for new children in school need to give information to the newcomers from other credible sources (who tend to be older children). Foster and Thompson (1991) give a detailed picture of the ways in which parents can be involved in the school's anti-bullying programme and approaches will be discussed later on in this book. Olweus (1993) also covers some useful strategies for involving parents, and the presentation of those initiatives to them. Evaluations of parental opinions of school's whole school behaviour policies and anti-bullying policies have demonstrated clearly that parents very much appreciate school's efforts and think it was high time that something was done (Trimingham, 1994 and Sharp, 1994).

## Some of the necessary features of an effective whole school policy

Implementing a whole school policy is one of the ways in which organisations can change, and so the process of implementation needs to be considered in the same way as the management of any kind of change. We discuss some of the detailed strategies for implementing whole school policies in later sections of this book – for now, let us consider some of the essential features of a whole school policy. Successful implementation of some kinds of policies can only be achieved with a general commitment to that policy from all members of the school community. All members are necessarily involved because the delivery of the policy depends upon them behaving in an appropriate way. They have to understand the reason as to why that particular action of theirs is necessary, when they should respond in that way, and – crucially – who else in the school community will act to back them up. If such policies are to be achieved, they need to be designed with maximum appreciation of those situations in which the 'average' member of the school community will need to apply the policy and the information to achieve this cannot be gathered without the active involvement at the policy design stage of those people on whom the implementation will rest. The reason for adoption of whole school policies in certain circumstances rests essentially on this social mechanism, not on any broader theory of management or social relations.

Accordingly, the whole school community needs to be actively involved in the processes of recognising the need for a policy, in consultation about the precise definitions as to what the policy covers, and what the agreed actions should be in different relevant circumstances. Different members of the school community will need to be involved in implementing the policy in different contexts. To put it at its simplest, teachers will need to know the agreed response to situations as they are brought to their notice and the children will need to know what actions the policy supports and does not support when they are playing amongst themselves. Similarly, parents will need to know the implications for their activities when they are involved through their children in incidents of bullying or tensions based around membership of different ethnic groups. Each of these groups brings their own concerns and situations to the process of working out a policy suitable for this particular school, and in doing so contributes to the effectiveness of the policy.

*Policy Limitations*

An important part of any whole school policy is its limitations. Nothing is ever capable of being expressed in such detail that all uncertainty can be removed, or every possible instance covered. Any policy will be a mixture of statements of agreed actions and procedures which would be generally applicable in a range of situations. Some of the situations may be crucial, and others relatively superficial. The views of the school community need to be sought as to which situations of implementation are to be concentrated on in the policy and which can be safely left to individual application of general principles. A policy without a number of key examples included will seem like another list of general admonishments, but a policy with every possible example included would be an impossible document to produce or to understand.

*Policy Ownership*

Detailed 'awareness raising' of issues, and consultation of the whole school community leads to the sense of ownership on the part of that community. They will feel that they have produced the policy through their joint efforts. This 'ownership' will be further validated by adoption of the policy by the whole school. This ownership again leads to emotional identification with both the goals of the policy and the acceptable behaviours described in the policy. In turn, implementation and continued involvement in the monitoring processes comes much more easily than it would do if they had not been so involved in the policy construction. The management's processes of dissemination of the policy are then received with understanding and approval, rather than the benign neglect with which so many school policies are received.

One implication of this process of development of a whole school policy is that the policy resulting is always specific to the actual individual people involved in this particular school at this particular time. Importing a well written section of another school's policy on the grounds that it looks complete and well worked out, will save time, but will totally nullify the advantages of having a whole school policy in the first place.

The general sections of the policy will have implications for the management of a number of school processes, as well as the specific issue being considered. Accordingly that small working group actually writing the policy from the various suggestions and documents received during the consultation process will need to consider such issues as:

- A clear definition of those situations being considered – using the example of bullying, just when do we consider that bullying is happening between children?
- A clear statement of the general principles governing acceptable behaviour in such circumstances.
- Some crucial detailed examples of how to apply those principles.
- The ways in which the appropriate behaviour can be emphasised, explained, and reinforced through the school curriculum – both the orthodox subject curricula and pastoral curriculum.
- Sanctions and discipline issues – although many examples of inappropriate behaviour may be minor, informal and be too numerous to involve a formal disciplinary process, at some point these infringements of general expectations of acceptable behaviour will spill over to the point where more formal disciplinary action is needed.
- The implications for staff development amongst the teaching and non-teaching staff.
- Different ways in which the policy might be monitored – how would we expect to observe the changes occurring after the implementation of the policy?

● Implications for the supervision system in the school. Bullying in particular, because it is so generally disapproved of by adults, tends to happen outside the obvious gaze of those people supervising children.

Not all these of course need to be included in the basic policy document for the school. Some of the general issues, for example staff development and possibly the pastoral curriculum issues, are centrally relevant to the involvement of the staff, as opposed to children or parents. Decisions need to be taken by the project management team and the school management as to the best way of writing and disseminating the policy so that those involved can perceive it most easily. However at this stage the writers should take care not to so heavily paraphrase all the suggestions and comments received during the consultation so as to make their contribution to the final document unrecognisable by those who made the suggestions. All the contributors need to be able to perceive how they have contributed by seeing at least some of their suggestions included.

A further general concern of the policy writers at this stage is also how can a policy be monitored and reviewed? This is essentially a management task, although again the review process needs to include elements of consultation with the various groups in the school community as to how they would wish to see the policy amended. Review is also a very appropriate time for repeated dissemination of the policy as it then stands, and gives an opportunity for the school management to both feed back information on the monitoring process and further engage the school community's energies in promoting the positive behaviours expected.

## Leadership initiatives in implementing whole school policies

Introducing a whole school policy on behavioural issues into schools is clearly a change in existing practice, in that more members of the school community are involved in the process than is usually the case with new school policies, and that involvement in the policy has implications for the way people are expected to behave in certain fairly clearly defined circumstances in schools involving unacceptable behaviour. Much has been written about managing change processes in schools, and I will only mention a few key elements here. More detailed and expansive commentaries on the process are easily available elsewhere (see, for example, Everaard and Morris, 1990, Dean, 1985, Handy, 1986, Everaard, 1989, Her Majesty's Inspectorate, 1977).

### Managing Change in Schools

Put very briefly indeed, encouraging change in organisations in a smooth effective way so that the organisation actually does change its practices rather than merely becomes confused for a short time and then reverts to its original habits, does involve a number of fairly systematic managerial emphases. These are:

1. Encouraging the expectation that change is inevitable, that the need for it will be recognised by systematic managerial initiatives, and that from time to time the organisation will learn to operate in slightly different ways. This might be either in order to achieve the same tasks more effectively, or to achieve successful completion of new tasks or of tasks which now have a higher priority than they had before.
2. Increasing the clarity of the internal communication systems. Any organisation which is interested in responding to change must be able to communicate inside itself effectively. Sub-groups of staff which have to be involved in the implementation of decisions need to be accessible to management for comment through representative systems of meetings and consultation, both for management to seek guidance on the details of implementation as well as for staff to learn of the basic need for new practices. This helps staff to understand fairly completely what those new practices should be and how they are different from the old ones.
3. Management needs to emphasise that the general staff support systems need to be as supportive of individual efforts as possible, where those efforts are intended to help the organisation meet its tasks in a genuine sense. This means that the appraisal system, the reward system and the various sanction systems should be seen to relate to the central need to achieve an effective organisation. The more that potentially helpful ideas and activities are ignored by the management structure, and the more that people feel that their efforts are not appreciated by that structure, the less commitment to organisational effectiveness and a useful response to change will be received back. Unfortunately this requirement is in itself quite difficult to achieve because personal egos at all levels in the organisation have a terrible habit of getting in the way, leading to lack of recognition of other peoples' efforts and ideas and on over dependence on personally produced ideas. There is no point in 'dreaming of systems so perfect that nobody needs to be good' as T.S. Elliott put it succinctly.

Any management of any school nowadays is very well aware of the need to have a school responsive to change, and will have supported developments to achieve these general organisational aims of various types, and with various degrees of effectiveness. How does the process of leadership express itself then, in developing whole school policies on acceptable behaviour in school?

*Leadership as a Diffuse Process in Organisations*

Students of management literature will have realised by now that the notion of leadership as being based on one person, or even one or two people, is a gross over-simplification when considering the processes of change of organisations. A diagrammatic representation of the school as an organisation will have one person as principal, although even then they are associated with an increasingly influential board of governors. Even though senior managers must understand the nature of leadership in organisations, they do not necessarily have to perform as leaders themselves in all aspects of school life. They will need to perform as leaders in some aspects of school life, but the idea of the all-purpose leader who can inspire others to effort, has a clear and communicable vision of the future, can handle committees like a master politician, and can also read a computer print-out of the budget statement is now, and always has been, something of a myth. Some headteachers may well steer through the implementation of a whole school policy on acceptable behaviour with energy, vision, and commitment; but some parts of that energy, vision and commitment may well come from other members of the school hierarchy who have the unconditional support of the head and the senior management team, expressed in a public way. Leadership in many issues in a complex organisation may originate from those staff members who have a specific knowledge of the processes concerned and may already be in organisational roles where they have responsibility for the initiation of policies in certain areas. It would be a strange organisation where this was not true. However, whereas such *'devolved responsibilities'* may work perfectly well with only minimal but definite endorsement from the senior management team in areas where they can be implemented by relatively few people, for successful implementation of a whole school policy the senior management team and the headteacher need to be specifically, visibly, and continuously committed to the success of the implementation of the policy.

After the headteacher, the senior management team, and any particular persons who may be involved as leaders in the establishment of a policy have accepted the aim of establishing the new approach, what steps in managerial terms need to be taken next? Detailed case studies will occur later in the book - for now let us consider some of the general principles and specific managerial tasks necessary to pursue policy implementation.

## Transition management-laying the ground work for a whole school policy

This stage of actual implementation of the change is known in management theory as *'transition management'* which some authors see as a distinct phase in the overall school management task (Everaard and Morris,

1990). When implementing management determined changes, this transition management stage has to be a fairly well controlled process, as the general school community have usually been only minimally involved in the development of the policy change being implemented. However when implementing a whole school policy, where the change is so managed as to gain the commitment and involvement of most of the school community, the transition management process is slightly different. There is a much larger place in both drawing up the details of the policy itself and of the methods of implementation of the policy, for comments, initiatives and activities contributed by many of the members of the school community. If possible all of the groups in school should be represented. A second difference between normal transition management and transition management of a whole school policy is that in normal transition management the benefits to be gained by the policy are often relatively distant from the day to day experience of the school staff and children. When whole school policies on behaviour management are being implemented, the benefits of the policy are fairly clear to a large proportion of the school community involved. The need to plan for *'motivation'* by the usual mixtures of incentives and sanctions is much less marked, at least regards rewards and sanctions for particular individuals. Where rewards and incentives are in order, they should apply to whole groups of the school community rather than to any particular individuals, as the process of implementation of the policy will be highly dependent on the involvement of many people in that implementation.

**Establishing common values**

In any typical account of project management these come fairly near the top, as it is simply assumed that the existing management of the organisation is the team which is expressing the values. However in implementing whole school policies, particularly on behavioural issues but also on other themes such as the linkage between educational progress and vocational training, there may well be other people in the school community who are extremely concerned about the issue and whose energies and commitments would be very valuable as a core part of the policy management process. Accordingly almost the first part of transition management for whole school policies is to identify the W.S.P project management team. This should include the headteacher, but should not necessarily expect that person to take a dominant or a time-consuming role. It should also include someone else from the orthodox school management team, who would be then expected to take a more dominant role in accordance with their existing responsibilities. The rest of the group however should include a small mix of people from different levels in the organisation, who are already convinced of the value of putting some energy into establishment of whole school policies on behaviour topics and if possible have previously held some roles in the school involving a certain amount of leadership. A representative group such as this also indicates to the school community the involvement of all of them in the process in a central way, and gives them colleagues who can carry their early supports or misgivings to the knowledge of the policy management group. Very valuable information on current practices, attitudes, and implementation issues is made accessible to the management process in this way.

## Clarifying possible aims and objectives

The first management task of this group is to detail possible aims and objectives, framed in such as way as to bear some relevance to the current situation and for some of the more tactical objectives to be achievable in the relatively near future. A group such as this needs to feel that progress is attainable and that the attainment of these tactical objectives is largely under the group's own control. Involvement and commitment flows from such process control. The precise extent and form of the aims and objectives will differ according to the instincts of the group members, but the essential feature is that the school can perceive from their deliberations and the public statements of various kinds resulting from them that the whole school policy project has a clear set of values and purposes which can be accepted and endorsed by the great majority of the school community.

### Establishing Present Needs for Change

Needs for changes in practice can come either from the aims and values and their implications for action, or can come from aspects of the current situation on the ground, either inside or outside school. The kind of need relevant when establishing whole school policies on standards of behaviour is that the school community upholds standards of behaviour which enable children to learn effectively. The entire school community would see this as self evident. However there are also other needs which may only become evident on more detailed examination of the situation. For example, the ordinary records of routine sanctions imposed on children who have disobeyed school rules may show that many of the children involved are subject to sanctions on repeated occasions. This usually goes unremarked in the school, indeed may almost be expected. However from the point of view of a sanctions policy it is clearly a highly unsatisfactory situation, as it means that the sanctions are not being effective in preventing further rule breaking by the same individuals. Even if we consider the sanctions not as attempts at re-education but as straightforward punishments they are still not being effective if there is intended to be anything of a deterrent effect in the idea of punishment. Repeated punishments of

the same children are not doing anything to prevent school rules being broken, they are not doing anything for the child, they are very likely to
involve time and energy on the part of at least some members of staff, to
no effect whatsoever. They may in fact be even less use than this, because
when a child learns to cope with the school sanctions without too much
difficulty that idea becomes part of the self-image, and the child may be
even more likely in future to become involved in situations where rules are
broken and sanctions are endured as a badge of achievement. Accordingly,
when looking at the needs for a change in existing policy towards school
behaviour, details such as this may highlight a need to change the way that
the current system operates so as to minimise repeated use of sanctions
with the same child.

Similarly another area which can easily be in need of amended practices
is the relationship between school staff and parents when children are
involved in aggressive incidents of any type in school. Every year most
schools lose approximately a quarter of their parents and take on an equal
number of new parents, who can represent potential resources, potential public relations ambassadors, and potential sources of pressure on school staff if
their views about behaviour to be expected in school are not the same as the
school's views. In many ways it would be surprising if any working group in
any school did not include the need to improve communication with parents
over behavioural standards expected in schools and if the part that parents
could play in maintaining them did not reach the agenda.

In addition, when behaviour policies in the specific areas are being considered, it becomes very useful to do some kind of a data collection to establish what is happening at present. In the case of bullying for example one of
the very early pressures on schools to adopt effective anti-bullying measures
is when they become aware by surveys of just how much bullying is taking
place in school at present (see Arora and Thompson, 1987).

## Managing resources

As with all management tasks, some thought has to be given to the
resources needed. Staff time and energy are the major resources needed for
implementing whole school policy in these behavioural areas, together
with a certain amount of training time for staff centrally involved. There
may be a need for a minimal amount of curricular material for work in the
citizenship and humanities areas which can be easily used to stress the
values of supportive behaviour towards one another and the relatively disastrous consequences of more aggressive alternatives. Even so the crucial
factor is often not what materials are used but which themes the staff tend
to concentrate on when teaching using existing material.

Much of the staff time and energy involved in the whole school policy,
particularly at the implementation stage and to a lesser extent in the plan-

ning stages, represents time which would have to be spent under the existing regime. It sometimes feels in school that an impossibly high proportion of staff time is taken up with emphasising acceptable standards of behaviour. One of the effects of adopting a whole school policy is to make that time more effective, in actually preventing a certain amount of disruption in schools with a consequent reduction in the overall staff energies spent in this area. Holding the necessary planning and consultation meetings during the policy development stages of the operation does undoubtedly involve more meeting time, although this can be kept relatively limited by setting a clear agenda and effective chairing. Effective meetings also leave the group members feeling they are not wasting their time. It is also useful to remember that different meetings, have quite different purposes in relationship to the evolution of a policy. Some might be seen as awareness raising meetings, some as consultation meetings where the important element is to receive suggestions without necessarily arguing them out from every angle. The meetings which are charged with the task of integrating suggestions and detailed planning are almost always quite small meetings of people with a high commitment to the task and a good understanding of the range of processes involved.

Managers also need to consider whether the staff training requirements will need significant resourcing. Most schools are familiar with the mix of observation visits, outside one day courses, and more school based training involving local L.E.A or H.E. trainers and consultants, which have characterised much of the educational developments over the last ten years. Managers are also undoubtedly aware that the effectiveness of many if not all training functions is determined by the extent to which the home organisation wishes to take the issue on board and genuinely discover new practices which can be understood and implemented by enough people to make a genuine difference to the life of the school. Working out a whole school policy is clearly a process which involves the bulk of the training emphasis being on the 'school based' end, although continued and detailed long term commitment from one or two people may be underpinned by a long course in higher education or possibly even a higher degree dissertation. The resourcing needed for this kind of training mix may be only minimal, as the 'staff cover' element may be avoided completely and if local consultants are used with a clear brief from the school. For example most schools have good contact with their local behaviour support service and their local educational psychological service. Even if the particular individuals linked with the school are not particularly involved in the issue of whole school policies for improved behaviour, an approach from the school to the principal of the support service as a whole, can easily produce a medium term staff training project involving other professionals who are more interested and experienced in the area of the behaviour policies. This kind of use of local trainers may even be completely free, the only expenses being the expenses of particular training materials if it is decided that some nationally based training package is appropriate. In the anti-bullying policy area at least, the D.F.E. plans to provide all schools in the country with awareness raising and training materials as a central free service. There are also other packages available nationally which are extremely cheap in training terms (Besag, 1992). By thinking through the training needs carefully and recognising that the best mode of training is very largely school based with some local consultancies, training expenses can be kept right down. Later on in the book we shall see the minimal extent of the training provided for schools in the Sheffield Anti-Bullying Project, and some comments of the teachers in the participating schools to their training needs at the end of the project.

**Managing the monitoring and review processes**

When first implementing any procedural changes, many managers are tempted to assume that once a change is made, it is made and the matter can be forgotten about. With increasing experience of managing however they realise that nothing can be further from the truth. For any change to be implemented, the change leaders need to set up a system for monitoring the new procedures, and for monitoring the actual outcomes of the changed procedures in terms of their effect on the core tasks of the school. Many monitoring processes start with the first aim, but omit to specify how the change is meant to improve the actual performance of the organisation, or to monitor these predicted changes to see if they in fact are occurring. Indeed many educationists would suspect that some change leaders would see such specific expectations for improved functioning as being at best unnecessary and at worst likely to be embarrassing. However, simply because whole school policies only work successfully if the whole school is genuinely involved in them, and because if the whole school is to be kept involved then they must be able to see that their efforts are achieving some useful change, it is important that those planning the whole school policy do look to the future and ask the key question *'how will we know if it is working?'*.

Such active plans to maintain and review policies are even more important when we consider the natural history of change in organisations. This was well illustrated by some recent work following up anti-bullying programmes in Scandinavia. Forty schools in one particular area of Norway had mounted a systematic anti-bullying policy, during the period when there was active support from a research team. During this period there was a marked reduction in bullying in the schools concerned. However when the research team went back to the same schools three years later, it appeared that only three of the forty schools had continued active support for the anti-bullying policy after the end of the research period. For all the schools as a whole, the average amount of victimisation had dropped by almost 50 per cent during the period of the active intervention. However, when assessed three years later the average level had climbed back to slightly above its original level. When the results from the forty schools were considered individually, those three schools which had actively maintained the policy over the intervening three years had maintained and slightly improved on their results at the end of the research intervention. The levels in the other schools had increased, bringing the average overall levels of bullying up to slightly above the pre-intervention baseline. The researchers concluded that if reductions in bullying were to be maintained and improved on over time, the policies themselves had to be reviewed, monitored and re-implemented over time also. They commented that *'the accidental now and then approach could possibly make the situation worse and not better'* (Roland, 1993).

This general conclusion is of course what we would logically expect, when considering the matter objectively. However it is inconvenient in the heat of planning new developments in schools to have to appreciate that if positive changes are to be maintained, the policies producing that change have to be reviewed and relaunched, and the amended practices have to be seen as the new orthodoxy in the life of the school.

The same research study did note however that the presence of a research team actively involved with the schools collecting data on the effectiveness of the change, was a sufficient incentive for schools in another part of Norway to maintain their programmes more actively. The monitoring and review question then becomes *'do schools need an external agency to encourage them to maintain a high profile for such behaviourally based intervention policies?'*. It is likely that some degree of external support will be given by the Inspectorate, either Central Government Inspectorate or the more frequent OFSTED team inspections, but it is quite uncertain how far such inspections will continue to be seen as supportive by schools as opposed to bureaucratic and basically an interference with normal school life. It will be possible to find external support nearer home, for example the local behaviour support service or educational psychology service would usually be pleased to assist schools to undertake monitoring and review projects.

## *Designing Monitoring Processes into the Whole School Policy*

As mentioned above there are three general types of data which can be used in monitoring policies. The first is actual changes in the behaviour and attitudes of people in the school; the second is the usual type of 'event' data collected routinely in schools; and the third is monitoring the occurrence of the procedures in the policy itself.

The question *'how will we know if the policy is working?'* is a good question to include in the various consultation processes, and children and other staff will suggest a range of ways in which the question can be answered. They may tend to concentrate on monitoring outcome behaviours. Suggestions people make, as well as methods used elsewhere, can generally be classified into two types of information gathering exercise. The first of these is the special survey, typically of children's opinions (as they are the ones most crucially affected by whole school policies of this type). Special surveys can be general opinion surveys (such as the 'Life in School' booklet initially used to assess the incidence of bullying) (Arora, 1994, in press), or they can be specific surveys perhaps covering a particular week in school life, when teachers may be asked to record all the instances of bullying which they come across. There are a range of possibilities for such surveys, which will be discussed in later chapters in this volume.

The other obvious way of assessing changing frequency of outcome behaviours is the regular management data which is collected as a matter of course in the school, such as those children suffering sanctions for aggression related breaches of school rules, or the number of occasions when parents are invited into school to discuss incidents of bullying and victimisation. Data of this kind may need slightly greater structuring than is inherent in current practice to ensure that information collected is specific enough to be clear, possibly through a simple coding system.

The third type of data, about the implementation of procedures in the whole school policy, will need to be specified at the same time as the whole school policy itself is specified, so that simple and appropriate recording systems are established. Some of these may be simply new classes of regular management data, such as parent involvement as mentioned above. Others may be specific only to the bullying policy itself, such as the establishment of records of children who complain of being bullied to teachers, with some indication of how frequently such children complain. This may be a specific procedure related to the schools pastoral care system, and be aimed at providing effective teacher support for particularly vulnerable children.

In general there are a large number of ways of monitoring both the outcome changes in behaviour expected and the effectiveness and degree of use of the procedures used, which are best worked out in each particular school. Data from other schools or other educational systems can sometimes give examples to be considered, but are unlikely themselves to provide the ideal way of doing it in any particular school wanting to set up monitoring processes. The procedures have to be tailored to fit the needs and preferences of the operating school.

### An Agenda for Monitoring Change

Let us take it that decisions have been made at the planning stage on what kind of information will be collected to monitor the change, both of the survey type and of the regular management data type. The next question is to identify people who will be responsible for the carrying out of the surveys or the collection of the regular event data, and in general who will co-ordinate the feedback from different parts of the policy system to write a review report. Such persons will need to report to a given body, ideally one which involves some outsiders to the school and which can ask for further information and suggest headings for the review report to consider. It should not be only this particular group of people (possibly the governors, possibly a general welfare committee with parental representation, possibly a specific committee set up by the parents' association) who see the report. After a review of the policy has been received and commented on by the reviewing group, then the whole school also needs to know an extent to which their efforts have been successful. This feedback process need not be elaborate – the general interest is such that even notices on noticeboards will be read.

When considering those people responsible for the review and reporting procedures, it is useful to bear in mind that those with the greatest motivation to actually keep the monitoring process properly structured may be those with the most to gain from an effective policy – hence the suggestion of parental involvement in the review body. The students themselves would be another group with a lot to gain, so perhaps the review body should also include one or two students.

### Re-emphasising the Policy Through Policy Developments

Re-stating most policies sufficiently often to remind people to implement them carries a great risk of merely boring the audience. Whole school behaviour policies have a great advantage over many other policies in this regard, as it is basically in the interests of all members of the school community that the policy is remembered. An integrated whole school policy for positive behaviour which combines elements of an anti-bullying policy, an anti-racist policy, and the behavioural elements of a special needs policy has yet a further advantage, in that the central themes of the policy can be approached from a number of different angles. These central themes of empathy with children from different groups, the social injustice of rejection, and operating inside an explicit value system, can be approached through the bullying issue, through the racism issues, and through the special needs issues. Even if these three themes are taken in strict rotation the variety inherent in the themes themselves are sufficient to avoid boredom or undue repetitions of single points. In addition of course the themes can be approached through different parts of the school system, for example through the tutorial system, through the curricular system, and through the disciplinary system. Such variety of mutually supporting themes and mutually supporting school systems should mean that re-statement of the policy is perfectly possible without the boredom becoming noticeable. The final secret weapon of course is that at the heart of a whole school policy is the issue of how can we be fair and just in our relations with one another, and how can anger and aggression be managed and controlled to enable normal human life to continue. These themes are central to much great literature, drama, and many modern soap operas, and appear by themselves to be among the least boring themes imaginable.

## Taking policies seriously

Children become adept at judging how seriously adults take what they are saying, and frequently observe differences between what adults say should happen in certain circumstances and what actually does happen, and where there are any such differences they take their cues from what does happen. The way that teachers implement supervision and sanctions demonstrates to the children just how important the school's anti-bullying policy is, because sanctions form one of the more constantly visible elements of that policy. The time that teachers give to preventative supervision and to sorting out incidents when the rules are broken will be taken by the children as a clear indication of the commitment of school to the policy. They are quite capable of distinguishing accurately between individual teachers in this regard, and will tend to trust certain teachers to be more effective in implementing the anti-bullying and discrimination policies than others. In all these areas of policy implementation the children who have been victims know how vulnerable they are to further aggression, and need to be able to trust the power structures in the school to behave appropriately when they are informed of specific problems. Minimising discrimination and bullying in schools depends on those children who are vulnerable having the confidence to approach members of staff, and feeling confident that their own personal situation after disclosures will be better than before. This means in turn that the skills which many school staff undoubtedly possess of combining discretion with firmness in approaching disciplinary situations need to be actively exercised. One of the interesting performance indicators of the policy in this area is the extent to which pupils will say on a random survey of attitudes, that if they were being discriminated against or victimised they would be prepared to tell a teacher. In schools with a high profile and successful anti-bullying policy, virtually all children will state spontaneously that their first preferred way of dealing with being bullied or being victimised is to tell a member of staff. In schools before such policies are developed, the proportion is nearer 30 per cent (Rigby and Slee, 1993, Thompson and Arora, 1991). In general, for the policy to be seen as serious and effective, the school staff have to be perceived as giving time to the problems raised by children in such a way as to encourage them and others to bring the problems to their notice before tensions build to such a point that damage is inevitable.

*Whole School Policies as Organisational Development*

Organisational development is a big phrase, with all kinds of grand and complex meanings. The very grandeur and complexity of the theme however gives it a somewhat mystical sound. When finally pinned down, textbooks of management tend to describe organisational development in terms such as planned efforts at improving the organisation's effectiveness, by aiming to make changes in the formal and informal procedures and norms of the organisation. It is usually intended to include improving the quality of life of the individuals in the organisation as well as improving the organisational performance. In many management texts, the theme tends to transform itself into the theme of the management of change in the organisation, with connotations that change is expected and necessary and will always tend to improve organisational effectiveness. During the 1980s and 1990s, many changes have been imposed on schools by changes in the pattern of administration of education nationally. However some changes can be identified and implemented by the organisation itself, if it so desires, to achieve outcomes actually desired by the school.

In many instances of organisational development – either of the large scale, externally imposed type, or the more locally instigated and managed type – so much attention is given to the nature of the changes that the anticipated improvements in performance of the organisation can easily become ill-defined or almost invisible. Implementing whole school policies to influence expected norms of behaviour between children, and between staff and children, is an example of precisely the right kind of organisational development – one with very clear outcomes, which can be assessed and monitored over time, and which have the approval of the vast majority of the school population. In addition, the procedures involved with the implementation of whole school behaviour policies have been demonstrated, in at least three different times and places, to have considerable impact on the incidence of bullying in schools – in a single detailed case study of a large secondary school in Yorkshire (Arora, 1994), in a large scale intervention project reported in Sheffield involving a mixture of primary and secondary schools (Smith and Sharp, 1994) and similar large scale intervention projects in Norway (Olweus, 1993 and Roland, 1993) as well as in a city-wide intervention project in the Midlands of England (Smith, 1994). As well as clearly demonstrating the extent of the changes possible, these projects also demonstrated some of the necessary factors in the schools implementing the policies to ensure effectiveness two of them had high correlations between the effectiveness of the policies and the extent of involvement of all the staff in the school with those policies (Smith and Sharp, 1994, Roland, 1993).

**Integrating the policies**

Although effective and genuine consultation can build support for the policies, the introduction of the policy has to have a clear initial relevance and impact. As mentioned above, it also has to be capable of being reviewed and refreshed over various time cycles in the life of the school, for example every year. When planning the implementation of an integrated whole school policy on acceptable behaviour which includes general school rules, specific anti-bullying policies, specific anti-racist policies, and specific inclusive education policies, it seems wise to phase the introduction of these different elements over a period of time. This is to limit the number and complexity of issues being discussed by pupils and staff at any one time, giving clearer and more easily managed consultation processes and policy formulations. For example, if the school concerned is one which already has a general positive behaviour programme which has not been specifically designed to cover the other three types of issue, then the extra issues can well be added to the positive behaviour programme at review points, maybe at the beginning or the end of a school year. The project management team would need to decide which of the three additional elements they wished to start with, bearing in mind particular circumstances of the school. Take for example a school which did have a higher proportion of children with statements of special educational need on campus, possibly because they were hosts to some kind of special unit or had extra resources for delivering education for children with special needs. It may make sense for that school to begin by focusing on the whole school behaviour policies necessary to achieve effective inclusion of the statemented children in the life of the school. On the other hand if there was a significant proportion of children from different ethnic backgrounds in school, then this area may be the higher priority. Alternatively if the school wished to begin with the area which probably has most instinctive general support from both pupils and teachers and parents, then they may decide to introduce the whole school anti-bullying policy as the first one of the three.

*The Relative Strength of Support for the Three Types of Behaviour Policy*

As was discussed in Chapter 1 much of the tensions arising in school around all these three issues can be traced back to tensions around the boundaries of social groups. Conversely, the key to reducing these tensions round the group boundaries comes from recognising that children and adults can communicate across the boundaries if there is an expectation that they can, if all the groups concerned do feel themselves to be part of the wider school community, and if the school activities give some assistance to that communication process across group boundaries. Accordingly, people from different ethnic groups have to realise both that they have many similarities with each other, and that their differences can be a source of interest and variety rather than ridicule and rejection. Similarly, the majority of children who are not involved with bullying either as victims or as bullies have to be helped to understand that members of their class groups and year groups who find themselves victims are there through no fault of their own, and the bullying can be minimised if they reject its occurrence and if they are assisted by the staff in so doing. For the children, the bottom line in acting against these relatively natural processes of group formation and discrimination is that they need to feel that the adults are on their side, as the aggression involved means that it can be personally risky to a greater or lesser extent to become involved actively. In the case of behaviour policies to support the integration of children with special needs, then there is usually a lot less direct antagonism and aggression (although statemented children do seem much more vulnerable to bullying than other mainstream children do) (Whitney and Smith, 1994, Nabuzoka et al, 1993).

Of these three areas, the one which we know is heavily supported by children is the anti-bullying stance. Rigby and Slee (1993) completed a detailed survey on children's attitudes towards other children across primary and secondary schools. The general conclusions were that between 60 and 86 per cent of children agree with statements such as *'I like it when someone stands up for kids who are bullied'*, *'It is a good thing to help children who cannot defend themselves'*, and *'It makes me angry when a kid is picked on without reason'*. This very high proportion of children rejecting victimisation in situations uncomplicated by different ethnic group membership maybe related to the relative ease of empathy for another child with apparently minimal differences from your own position. Hazzan (1990) found that one of the major causes of stress in six year-old children attending infant school was observing other children being picked on and being victimised. With children either who have very obvious special needs or who are clearly from a different background of some sort, this immediate empathy is probably less possible, as it becomes easier for the observer to say *'they're not like me'*.

The project management team then needs to decide which of the three specific policies to adopt first, and then which to include at a later review stage. Given other pressures, yearly reviews seem the obvious pattern.

One of the interesting results from the evaluation of the Sheffield anti bullying intervention project was that most of the school staff involved with the project felt that the anti-bullying policy should be seen as something different from the existing behaviour policy in school, but should be related to it. In general, the teachers felt that if the anti-bullying policy had been completely subsumed under the general school behaviour policy, much of the specific concern and urgency of the anti-bullying policy would have been lost. Handled in this sequential way, it becomes possible for schools to relate their specific policies to each other and to the overall positive behaviour policy in school, but at the same time not lose the particular impact of the individual policy. Having a new and particular focus at policy review time makes it possible to maintain some of the emotional novelty in the general policy for staff and students alike.

## From the whole school to the individual

The successful implementation of whole school behaviour policies depends on the behaviour of individual members of staff. Every school is, of course, made up of individuals and each of these individual members of staff will have developed their own unique approach to student behaviour. However, there are certain features of personal style which seem to contribute to more effective behaviour management skills.

Firstly, staff must be able to distinguish between 'control' and 'management'. Control can be achieved through fear or bribery and does not relate to good practice. It provides students with an effective but destructive model of relationship skills. The adult who is an effective student manager is usually consistently clear and firm in distinguishing between acceptable and unacceptable behaviour. These tight and explicit boundaries are established from the outset of the student/teacher relationship and are regularly reinforced. Any transgressions are responded to immediately and assertively but not aggressively. Within these parameters, however, a wide range of behaviours are viewed as acceptable and the teacher is able to be flexible in their interactional style with individual and groups of students. Social issues which emerge are discussed in a comfortable and sensitive manner, avoiding censorship and over-reaction. All students are overtly valued, even though their behaviour may be viewed as inappropriate. Indeed, this kind of teacher will have the ability and the willingness to see the logic in student behaviour, recognising that whilst some students may behave in a dangerous, annoying or inappropriate manner such behaviour is rarely 'bad' and rarely 'random'. Underlying this kind of approach is an implicit belief in the importance of and possibility for equality and constructiveness in relationships.

This set of qualities and skills can be encouraged and developed within all staff. Senior managers can actively promote an effective management style in staff through training, direct feedback and through staff selection criteria.

# CHAPTER 4

# Principles and Materials for Curriculum Interventions

One of the elements of effective implementation of whole school behaviour policies is using the curriculum to emphasise knowledge of effects of dissemination in its various forms. Before developing curriculum approaches, the project management group will need to consider if staff concerned need any training, using the staff development and training guidelines outlined in a later section. One possible area of need may be, for example, training in using discussion based teaching methods to explore values expressed by curriculum materials.

*The Psychological Significance of Curriculum Based Materials and Activities*

Education is basically about society's efforts to help children to identify, analyse, and understand the world around them. As well as understanding, education hopes to involve the children in the community emotionally, and gives them some of the attainments and skills to take part in that community themselves. The design and implementation of a whole school policy on bullying and the other specific themes in fact extends the areas of concern which the community is putting on the agenda for children's learning. One of the most natural learning mechanisms for children is observation and imitation, combined then with an intellectual analysis and critique of what has been observed. What has not been fully understood until recently however is the importance of the child's self-image in their understanding. Children look at the world around them and then interpret it in the light of their own understanding of themselves and their part in that world. Children construct their own sense of self from their experiences in understanding and taking part in their immediate community, and then sub-sequent information and ideas are interpreted from the position of that particular sense of self. When stories, plays, and even policies are presented to children in a way which invites their engagement and participation, the children can incorporate the themes and models into their emerging sense of self: The themes and possibilities become personalised, and children learn to say and believe *'I can feel more relaxed and less threatened by older children who might hurt me if I stay with my friends at dinner-time'* or *'I know how to argue along with my friends against someone who is bullying a younger child'*. Stories, plays, and policies demonstrate how these things can be done, and make it possible for children to participate in these social processes.

The general thrust of the curriculum implications of whole school behaviour policies are:

1. To raise awareness amongst the children of the existence of the problem from the point of view of those discriminated against and those bystanders caught up in the aggressive incidents.
2. To increase awareness of the damage done to the social group by the existence of such tensions.
3. To provide material illustrating the concerns and emotional reactions of those excluded or discriminated against.
4. To draw attention to the basic unacceptability of processes of discrimination and rejection of people purely as a result of not being a member of any given social group on grounds of social justice.

In practice very many of these themes come up in the humanities curriculum particularly in literary, historical, religious, and geographical studies. The threads of discrimination, violence and social disruption weave their way through much historical and contemporary reality.

The second general opportunity for the curriculum work related to whole school behaviour policies is the pastoral curriculum – sometimes described as personal, social and health education, commonly forming a curriculum spine for form tutor group work in tutor periods. Many schools have developed their own pastoral curriculum, depending on their own needs and the views of those involved in the tutoring structure. Others use commercially available materials. The more informal setting, and in particular the increased possibilities for a personal relationship between the form tutor and a particular group of children can give greater opportunity for approaching emotionally based and sensitive issues of direct concern to the group of children. Not all teachers acting as form tutors are comfortable in such teaching situations however and thought may need to be given to the whole issue of staff development in this area for pastoral care team members.

One aspect of awareness raising for teachers and for subject departments in schools is to identify the points in the particular curriculum taught by departments and individuals where the principles behind whole school behaviour policy can be emphasised. This can form part of a general curriculum audit for cross-curricular themes. The teaching staff do not need to spend anymore time on these topics, but need to emphasise when dealing with them in the course of the ordinary subject curriculum, the questions:

1. *'What was it like for the victim?'*
2. *'Was it right or just that these things occurred?'*
3. *'What effect did these events have on the wider community at that time?'*
4. *'How could this situation have been avoided?'*

Apart from any concerns of the whole school policy, asking such questions can serve to increase children's interest and involvement in the topics themselves, as well as their memory for the events.

## Specific themes relevant for particular whole school policies

Inside the general envelope of increased understanding of other people's situations implied by the general guidelines above, much specific material has been developed by schools in each of the three areas of concern. The following discussion will mention some of these.

### Curricular Themes for Multi-cultural and Anti-racist Policies

Much has been written in the more specialist literature about multi-cultural and anti-racist education, and in this section the intention is only to outline the basic principles behind such curricular interventions so that they can be translated into practice in a way appropriate for a particular school. These are based on an understanding of tensions which exist between groups of children and between adults and children, drawing on understandings of formation of social identity, the importance of group identification in that process, and the possibility of social influence.

There are three central themes underpinning an anti-racist curriculum:

1. Helping pupils become aware of the strength of their own developing identity, both as they see it and as other people see it.
2. Helping the students to become aware that they have many more similarities with people of their own age from different cultural backgrounds than they might at first assume, but that these similarities only become apparent when some communication is established.
3. Demonstrating that the undoubted differences which do exist between people from different cultural and ethnic backgrounds are real differences, but can be seen in certain contexts as providing interest and novelty in a social environment rather than meaning a threat.

These three themes are based upon the idea that how groups of people respond to each other is partly the responsibility of their own leaders, and partly that of leaders of the broader community of which the groups are apart. Furthermore, the consequences of seeing members of different groups as a threat and rejecting them on that basis is the beginning of a spiral which can lead to incalculable social damage. Quite apart from ethical and moral considerations, the bottom line in the rationality of anti-racism is sheer self preservation. The history of central Europe between 1933 and 1945, and the history of Yugoslavia from 1945 to 1993 give very clear pictures of patterns of social disintegration occurring when racist attitudes are accepted by community leaders as inevitable. There is of course a poignant example even closer to home, which is as yet very much unresolved, and soaks up millions of pounds of taxpayers money and a significant part of the British Armed Forces every year.

As with all curricula, anti-racist themes have both a cognitive and an emotional component. The easiest part to teach is of course the cognitive part, but for the teaching to be effective in terms of a positive behaviour policy the emotional part has to be developed in parallel. At the very least, emotional engagement needs group discussion by the students. If the class teacher is used to group work with children, then more active discussions, role play and active tutorial games can effectively involve the students on an emotional level. Using this combination of methods, tailored to suit the teaching styles of the particular individual teachers involved, it is possible:

1. To help students understand the significance of self identity contrasted with a stereotyped, inaccurate view of other people's identity.
2. To help students become aware of the many ways in which people can be different, and to identify how they are themselves unique.
3. To help students recognise how many different groups they are members of, and how they behave differently in each group. Students need to understand that self identity is a combination of different identities in different settings. We are always similar to some people and have some differences from others, but we can move from one group which is defined by one principle to another group defined by another principle quite easily, and in fact are doing this quite frequently every day.
4. By helping the students to become aware that groups have symbols, and group membership can be both acknowledged and actively advertised through the use of such symbols. Dress of course provides a very rich source of symbols and one which the students will readily identify with. Hairstyles may well be another. Words can also be symbols – slogans, definitions of social groups, and even attributes can be seen as symbols. For example who is meant by 'they're taking our jobs'?
5. The curriculum should help students become aware of some of the positive and negative consequences of being 'different', with respect to a number of different group memberships. This can be done by enquiring about the positive and negative effects of being say a young people in a group of adults, a boy in a group of girls, a white person in a group of black people,

or someone who lives in the country with a group of people who live in the city. This helps students to become more aware of the emotional and other consequences of being 'different' and hence to empathise more with people who are members of different groups from themselves.

6. To help the students recognise the way stereotypes work. This includes understanding how to acknowledge people as members of particular groups. Stereotyped perceptions of people assume that they will always behave in a certain manner. It hinders recognition of the differences between individual members of that group and similarities between members of that group and members of the perceiver's group. It is also possible to ask questions about whether the children actually do agree with the 'stereotype' often associated with particular groups, and what they think about that difference.

7. The curriculum can help students become aware of how particular views about people from different backgrounds were formed. Activities round this theme can be focussed directly on the multi-cultural issue, or they can relate to views about a number of other kinds of group membership. For example activities and discussion might focus on what experiences were important in forming the students' perception of people from a different country such as France or India, or it could focus on experiences which were influential on forming ideas about the opposite sex, or of policemen, or of travellers. Whatever the children choose to concentrate on, such activities help the students to understand the way in which their own perceptions of other people belonging to different groups have been influenced by particular personal experiences. They can learn that their experiences may vary from those of other students, or may have been influenced not by any direct experiences at all, but by representations of the others in the media.

The Swann Report (1985) gives six criteria to help teachers look critically at the curriculum being offered, in order to help them judge how far their present curricula does reflect some of the principles of a curriculum for a multi-cultural community. These are:

1. The variety of social, cultural and ethnic groups and a perspective of the world should be evident in visuals, stories, conversation and information.
2. People from social, cultural and ethnic groups should be presented as individuals with every human attribute.
3. Cultures should be empathetically described in their own terms and not judged against some notion of 'ethno-centric' or 'euro-centric' culture.
4. The curriculum should include accurate information on racial and cultural differences and similarities.
5. All children should be encouraged to see the cultural diversity of our society in a positive light.

6. The issue of racism at both institutional and individual level should be considered openly and efforts made to counter it.

Failure to meet these criteria will have a negative effect on all students, regardless of race or culture. An unbalanced view of cultural diversity, which focuses overwhelmingly on one or two cultures, will alienate students, parents and teachers from under-represented cultures and may even damage the development of their identity (Maxime, 1994). It will provide students whose culture is over-represented with a distorted picture of humankind and will encourage discrimination and bias in relationships. Just as when tackling gender bias teachers have deliberately set out to use non-sexist language and to promote positive images of both men and women, similar efforts must be made to promote positive images of all cultures through choice of language, literature, historical or political figures, inventions and initiatives. Banks (1994), in discussing identity work with black children, recommends 'The A-Z of Black People in Science and History' by Forde et al (1988) as a good resource book for teachers of younger students. Maxime (1987a, 1987b) has produced two workbooks which provide materials for identity work with black youngsters.

Any discussion of curriculum content in the early 1 990s is not complete without at least a passing mention of the 'National Curriculum'. Even within this subject centred framework, there will still be intention on the part of the government to maintain some space for personal and social education and matters such as education for a multi-cultural society. The National Curriculum Council has issued some guidance on these matters (NCC, 1989/1993). The 1989 circular saw personal and social education, including multi-cultural education and other pastoral topics, as part of the 'whole curriculum' and in particular as examples of cross-curricular dimensions.

'These (cross-curricular dimensions) are concerned with the intentional promotion of personal and social development. Whilst secondary schools may offer courses of personal and social education, it is the responsibility of all teachers and is equally important in all phases of education. Major cross-curricular dimensions include equal opportunities, and education for life in a multi-cultural society. They require the development of positive attitudes in all staff and pupils towards cultural diversity gender equality and people with disabilities.'

Keen observers of the implementation of the national curriculum however will undoubtedly have noticed that the statutory requirements and non-statutory guidance for the three core subjects almost totally ignore possibilities for introducing themes relating to the cross-curricular dimensions in general. Unlike the core and foundation subjects these cross-curricular dimensions are not subject to statutory control, so at present individual schools have a choice as to how far they should include such themes in the teaching. The government's view is clearly that each school must choose for itself what it's own priorities are in these areas.

There has been a considerable amount of educational literature in recent years which have been devoted to attempts to fill out detail and provide material for multi-cultural and anti-racist curriculum content which is relevant to the whole curriculum. With the advent of the national curriculum this support will continue for teachers and schools who are so concerned. Existing guides which are accessible for the non-specialist include Nixon (1985), Gillborn (1990), Arora and Duncan (1986), Grugeon and Woods (1990), Gill and Levidow (eds) (1987). A journal called 'Multi-Cultural Teaching' (published by Trentham Press, Stoke-onTrent) publishes many interesting and short articles of direct relevance to classroom teachers. For teachers wishing to follow up in detail some of the possible variations between the way that different schools treat multi-cultural education, Smith and Tomlinson (1989) provide a good introduction.

**Specific curriculum elements for an anti-bullying whole school policy**

The basic principles of the curriculum interventions for an anti-bullying policy are fairly similar to those underlying interventions with anti-racist policies discussed above. The exact mechanism is clearly different from racism, so the detailed intervention strategies have distinct content whilst sharing some general principles. We saw in chapter 2 that bullying itself has its roots in four parallel processes, which were:

1. The use of or threat of aggression and violence, or the threat of aggression and violence by someone in order to boost their own social status with their peer group, where both the bully and the peer group accept that aggression is a perfectly normal and acceptable part of everyday social life.
2. The vulnerability of the potential victim to such random violence or threat of violence, due primarily to their lack of social support and difficulty in making active and assertive social relationships with peers.
3. The relative lack of involvement of the bystanders, who would compose the great majority of the children who are aware of the bullying, largely from a fear of getting involved in potentially aggressive situations and a lack of any clear set of principles as to what they might do and how they might do it.
4. The lack of a clear set of values and principles from the wider community which might make it clear both that bullying is unacceptable to that wider community and what the bystanders should do.

Viewed in this way, it is clear that controlling bullying is in essence a social control activity, but one which is a very consistent part of the wider set of values that the community expects schools to pass on to the children. In this sense, the school's anti-bullying policy reinforces the transmission of social values from parent to child, except that in those instances where social values concerned with the unreasonable use of aggression have not been a part of the child's upbringing, then the school is perhaps a prime socialisation agent involved with that task. The school can propagate such values, because the size of the school community is such that the damage that can be done by unreasonable use of aggression and violence is clearly seen by the children, and it is a large enough community to exert direct social pressure on those who bully. The school is also aided by the developmental changes taking place during childhood and adolescence, which include those of learning to make friends more effectively, and increasing skills in handling aggression from other members of the group. A clear lead from the adults in the school is crucially necessary to state and propagate the anti-bullying ethos of the whole school policy. This is a vital social context for the inclusion of material in the curriculum which can give children the opportunity to develop arguments, attitudes and skills to handle incidents of bullying, and some chance to rehearse them in public. Attitudes can be seen as 'in the head opinions', but are very difficult to define and also quite unstable before they are expressed in a coherent way in a public forum. It's not enough for schools to leave children with a general impression that bullying is wrong, as this will not be effective in giving the children useful convictions and skills in avoiding bullying themselves and minimising it in their community. The work has to be taken further, to the point where children are given the actual opportunity to practise explaining why bullying is wrong, and to practise saying and doing the kinds of things they need to say and do in order to maintain anti-bullying values amongst their peer group.

Reading the above, some educationists may wonder how far these principles are common to whole school behaviour policies in the other specific areas mentioned. On many occasions, the principles do overlap to a great extent. In order to teach them effectively, however, teachers have to present issues in specific situations, and so for the curriculum work the three types of behaviour policy have been presented as separate themes here.

*Anti-bullying Curricular Topics in Foundation Subjects and Personal Social Education*

Most of the obvious opportunities for mentioning anti-bullying themes during the teaching of the core and foundation subjects fall in the general area of the humanities. The general themes to be explored are those complementary to the routes of bullying as described above. These are:

1. Understanding an empathy for vulnerable individuals, particularly in situations where they are being victimised through unjust aggression or threat of aggression.

2. Discussion and if necessary debate round the issue of what forms of aggression are acceptable in a community and what reasons can be given for the acceptability of aggression under certain circumstances?
3. What should the bystanders say and do when they find themselves part of a community where bullying is taking place? How can they support each other and in turn gain support from appropriate points in the wider community?

As with anti-racist curricular themes, themes of the inappropriate use of aggression and violence occur all too frequently throughout the world's cultures – it may even be said that this is one of the two great themes. The extra input from school and the school staff is to give a greater significance to the implications of the themes that are already there, rather than necessarily introduce new ones. School staff do need to take up a 'committed' position on this issue, although it is a commitment that would be heartily approved of by the entire wider community. The point of discussing 'when might aggression be acceptable' is to enable the children to discover, learn about, and be able to express a specific moral position, i.e. that aggression is a damaging and often unnecessary part of mankind's emotional life, which is only justified under conditions of great threat or danger, and is to be minimised wherever possible.

In recent years there has been much curricular material specifically prepared for those situations where teachers wish to work from new material. Given the straight jacket of the national curriculum, in many subjects the introduction of completely new material will be somewhat limited, which is why teachers need a general understanding of the principles discussed above. Discussion arising from these principles can find their way into almost any of the traditional humanities subjects, even using existing national curriculum material. Extra material is readily available, and has been excellently reviewed with detailed discussions on the best ways of using them by Sharp and Smith (1994).

The pastoral curriculum, sometimes labelled personal and social education or personal, social and health education, was increasingly used by schools before the advent of the national curriculum as a basis for tutor group activities. Some schools have managed to maintain some elements of it, and if the proportion of time allocated to the core and foundations subjects is reduced over the next few years, then it is possible that more schools will be able to find more time for it. Teaching activities in the pastoral curriculum are often group work based, and this does raise all the old issues about forms of support and staff development for those members of staff who find themselves operating as form tutors but whose preferred style of teaching is basically information giving and didactic. This question will be considered in some more detail in the chapter on in-service training, but many school managers would expect that the usual style of teaching in form tutor periods would probably be discussion based with a reasonable amount of structuring from the form tutor, rather than more explicitly group work based. It is perfectly possible to do useful anti-bullying curriculum work in tutor groups from such a basis, although using more group work methods such as project work, and problem solving groups, as well as activity based groups using drama as a tool, would be likely to have a greater impact on individual children's attitudes and would be likely to give them more new skills to actually use on the playground.

## *Issues to be Approached with Children in Tutorial Groups*

The tutor group is an obvious place to begin when consulting the children about the details of an anti-bullying whole school policy in secondary schools. Such consultations would usually come with a strong element of leadership from the school and hence from the form tutor, to the effect that the school is going to strengthen its behaviour policies to include specific anti-bullying practices, and would like the children's help in clarifying and specifying what these might be. In primary schools, most children are in classes where they have a long-standing relationship with the teacher, and so these issues can be raised in the usual class group. Issues initially raised would then include:

1. What the children mean by bullying and how they can define it in practice. The school policy planning group may well have decided to put forward a full definition of bullying as a part of its policy. If it has, then this phase of the discussion may be used to elaborate the school's definition.
2. Where does bullying occur? Useful distinctions here are in class, on the playground and corridors, out of school.
3. What are the effects of bullying, for the children involved and for the bystanders?
4. What can the school do to reduce bullying? This will be likely to produce fluent debate and comment from most groups of children, and will include suggestions for improving the level of supervision in the school, for ways of responding to bullying, and possibly for teachers to take the issue more seriously and more sensitively. They may raise for themselves the issue of what can the bystanders do, or the teacher may need to raise it.
5. How can the school assess how much bullying is taking place? They may have a general notion of doing surveys, and the question of the form of surveys then provides a useful topic for small group work.

One essential step for the teacher both during and after such discuss would be to take note of some of the more specific ideas for prevention, and convey them back to the whole school policy planning group. If the children are sufficiently mature, it may be possible to appoint one of them to do this. With older children, it may even form the focus of a project for one particular group.

## Non-violent Conflict Resolution

The main aim of any kind of behaviour policy must be to improve the way in which children and adults relate to each other. To achieve this we may need to specifically teach children how to manage their relationships more effectively. Indeed, we would argue that this teaching is essential if the policy is to be implemented by students.

Some aspects of relationship skills, such as being co-operative and friendship building, are promoted throughout education. However, this is only partially equipping children for the range of interactions they are likely to encounter. It is unrealistic to expect children (or adults) to be 'friends' all of the time. On a broader scale, all of us build a continuum, of relationships and there are inevitably some people we prefer to be with more often than others. Our preferences do not however justify discrimination or aggression. We need to help children to understand the reasons behind their preferences and to challenge those which are based on stereotype or ignorance. Children can be taught to enjoy difference and diversity. This can be achieved by deliberately setting out to establish a caring student community. Kreidler (1990) describes the 'peaceful classroom' which is based upon five core qualities. These qualities are

1. *Co-operation:* Pupils learn to work together, to trust, to help and share with each other;
2. *Communication:* Pupils learn to observe more carefully, communicate needs and wants and listen sensitively;
3. *Positive emotional expression:* Pupils learn to express their feelings (including anger, fear and frustration) in ways which are not aggressive or destructive;
4. *Appreciation for diversity:* Pupils learnt to respect and appreciate difference and similarities and to understand how prejudice works;
5. *Conflict resolution:* Children learn the skills of responding creatively to conflict.

In all relationships, some degree of conflict is inevitable. The scale of this conflict can vary from a difference of opinion to war. DeCecco and Richards (1974) studied ways in which 8,000 students coped with conflict. They found that most students, regardless of school or family background, ignored or avoided conflict situations. They noted that these kinds of coping strategies often lead to tension and misdirected aggression. Unless taught otherwise, children will tend to resolve conflict by using bullying, violence or manipulation.

If we are to help children manage their relationships with others more constructively we should avoid four assumptions. Firstly, we should recognise that children do not come to school already equipped to handle more difficult aspects of relationships. We need to teach them how to do this. Secondly, we ourselves should feel more comfortable with conflict, recognising that conflict itself is not a 'bad thing' but how we handle it can effect our experiences of it. Thirdly, we need to view conflict as a problem to be solved rather than a contest to be won. This shift in attitude helps us to avoid competitive, inflexible stances where one person or group 'wins' and another 'loses' and therefore makes a mutually acceptable 'win-win' outcome more likely. Finally, we need to appreciate that there are a range of conflict resolution styles. Whilst there is no 'right' way to resolve conflict, some approaches to conflict are more likely to lead to a positive, constructive outcome than others.

Children often come to school with a tendency towards one of two conflict styles: fight or flight. If a child uses 'fight' strategies they are likely to respond aggressively to conflict, either verbally or physically or in some other way to 'beat' their opponent. Alternatively, when a child takes 'flight' from a conflict then they may ignore or avoid a situation even to the extent of breaking off a relationship or missing school. They may repress what they actually feel and deny that a problem exists. This is a common response if the child is afraid that they might lose or believe that conflict is wrong. Sometimes, a 'fight' or a 'flight' response may be the appropriate one. If a brick is about to fall on a child's head, then their friend may justifiably forcibly push them out of the way. If a stranger tries to drag a child into a car, they should struggle to escape. However, often aggressive or passive approaches do not effectively resolve the conflict. They can foster resentment and helplessness within the children, are usually frowned upon by adults and are often in direct contravention of the school code of conduct or behaviour policy.

To be able to resolve conflict constructively, children need to understand what conflict is and how it can lead to either positive or negative outcomes. They also need to recognise the value of a positive outcome for themselves and for others so that they will be willing to implement creative conflict resolution strategies. Finally, they need to learn and practise the basic skills involved in constructive conflict management: active listening and assertiveness. Direct teaching of these essential communication skills can in itself iron out many minor disagreements and help children to manage their relationships with others. Outbursts of aggressive behaviour, bullying and harassment often reflect a child's ignorance of other ways of expressing anger, fear or frustration or their lack of experience in negotiation or discussion.

Once children have learned to be effective listeners and to express their feelings and needs in a clear, direct and honest way, they can be introduced to conflict resolution procedures. These usually involve both parties saying what they want and why they want it (and being listened to carefully). Conflicts can escalate at this stage because although clear about what they *want* to happen, the children do not state what they *need* to happen. Successful conflict resolution usually occurs when both parties *needs* are met. Having established wants and needs, they then brainstorm possible solutions. Both parties finally agree on the most suitable solution and put it into practice. There are numerous resources available for teachers who want to know how to teach children these kinds of skills. One good example is William J Kreidler's (1984) 'Creative Conflict Resolution' .

## *Co-ordination of Curricular Coverage Between Subject Areas and Tutor Groups*

Many schools are familiar with the task of completing a curriculum audit for the cross-curricular themes. The whole school policy project management group may decide to co-ordinate the coverage between tutor groups and subject teachers. The easiest way to achieve this may be to specify what activities should be covered in the tutor groups, and then to indicate other issues with examples for the subject teachers to consider. The extent of this process is dependent on the existing structure for curriculum discussion and review within and between subject areas existing at the moment. Where effective mechanisms exist, then the project management group may need do nothing other than indicate questions.

## *Supportive Materials for Curricular Discussions on Anti-bullying Policies*

During the past couple of years there has been more and more assistance available for schools interested in curricular materials for supporting whole school policies. School staff do find such materials very helpful, and so one of the first acts of the W.S.P. project management group should be to purchase some of these. The most usual form of materials is a video recording, around certain issues often involving children's drama, with accompanying sets of teacher's notes and other suggestions for policy development. Many are only intended to be outline supports, and many of them have been designed to be used with children of particular ages. One of the most extensive and up to date reviews of these materials is included in a recent book on intervention in bullying (Sharp and Smith, 1994), and this volume would be very useful for the school to purchase at this stage of the project. At a slighter greater level of generality, Smith and Thompson (1991) gives a range of case studies of projects in schools written by the teachers themselves which have been used as a part of whole school policies. The Journal of the National Association for Pastoral Care in Education, 'Pastoral Care in Education', has in recent years had a series of teacher focused articles on assessing the incidence of bullying and various intervention strategies.

For those wishing to send off their cheques immediately, the following four video based packs have been highly recommended from a number of sources. For primary schools, Central Independent Television (1990) have produced a video *The Trouble with Tom* and Kumar (1985) has produced a set of story materials for use in the classroom called *The Heartstone Odyssey.* For secondary pupils, Central Independent Television again (1990) produced the video *Sticks and Stones,* and the Neti-Neti Theatre Company (1990) produced the video *Only Playing Miss!* two of the members of that theatre group, Cassdagli and Gobey (1990), have produced a written version of the script and elaborations for other dramatic work round the same issue. One of the case studies in Smith and Thompson (1991) is in fact a case study of the use of this material by this theatre group (Gobey, 1991 and Housden, 1991).

## Supporting inclusive education whole school behaviour policies through the curriculum

In earlier chapters the difficulties faced by pupils with some degree of special need, and by their teachers in effectively including them within mainstream education were outlined. Such children are much more likely to become victims of bullying and other discrimination than are children without any special needs (Thompson, Whitney and Smith, 1994). Teachers face many of the same problems in making judgements about the appropriateness of children's behaviour as they deal with the children everyday, as they do with the more obvious behavioural tensions to do with racism and bullying. The dilemmas for the teachers dealing with children with special needs, whether of the more severe 'statemented' type or the other 16 per cent of children who may have special needs at some time in their school career, is basically expressed as *'how far should I make allowances for the extra difficulties this child has?'* In many schools teachers make these decisions on the hoof on the basis of their knowledge of the children concerned and the strength of their relationship with them. Most schools have a small core of staff who are specifically concerned with children who have special needs, and informal classroom discussion can often help teachers to make those judgements consistently and reasonably. The main thrust of whole school behaviour policies to support inclusive education is to help teachers and children behave in a consistently appropriate way towards those members of their community with some degree of disability, whether more or less severe.

The role of special needs policies has been emphasised by the 1993

Education Act and the Code of Practice. Governors and school managers are now expected to ensure that all children with some degree of special needs are identified by the school staff, and that provision is made for those needs in school or through the agency of the Local Education Authority. Over the next few years this will lead to all schools strengthening their general policies to identify and provide for the needs of such special children. A whole school behaviour policy for inclusive education of children with special needs provides understanding and guidelines for appropriate standards of behaviour for them, for the other pupils and staff towards them. In practice the issue of what are appropriate behaviour expectations for children with special needs will arise fairly frequently through their increased tendency to find themselves as victims of bullying, and also through the likelihood they will have increased difficulties in learning social skills. In the Sheffield Anti-bullying Intervention Project, over half of the children with special needs felt that they were victims of bullying in schools, and this was approximately corroborated by the special needs teachers in their schools.

*Preliminary Issues for the Whole School Policy Project Management Group*

Before considering the specific issue of the curricular approach to whole school policies for inclusive education, there are a number of background issues which the project management group will need to consider. These are to do largely with clarifying in their own mind the background principles of the policy. They will need to consider such issues as:

– how to keep separate for staff concerned with the identification and provision for children with special needs (the usual meaning of 'special needs policy'), the issues of behavioural standards expected from the children so specifically identified; and,
– the more general issues for the children, concerned with appropriate behaviour and reasons for it when they are with people with special, needs.

If the two processes are not kept separate, the school is in danger of strengthening even further the 'disabled' identity of the children whom the school has identified as having special needs for purely educational purposes.

The whole school special needs behaviour policy crucially depends on the school community coming to a clear idea as to what should constitute special needs for these purposes. The W.S.P. project management group needs to think these questions through also, and recognise the inevitability of the definition of special needs remaining in the hands of the handicapped person themselves, either through explicit recognition and request for help on particular matters, or through demonstrating an obvious inability to cope with particular circumstances. If the children really cannot cope, then some degree of special arrangements will need to be made to enable them to participate in the life of the school. If the former, the person who is disabled themself specifies the nature of the changes, to meet the particular need identified. This particular definition then leads children on to realise that this is basically the 'all children are special' definition, where the general standards of behaviour expect that all of us have our own needs from time to time, which we hope those around us will recognise or will respond to us when we tell them. In this sense, we all have special needs, and the problem of the stereotyped perception leading to exclusion of particular individuals because they are seen to belong to a different group disappears, in principle at least.

For the actual implementation of the educational special needs policy, as distinct from the whole school behaviour policy for inclusive education, the staff are clearly working with the second half of the definition above. They are alerted by the obvious difficulty certain children have in completing educational tasks, and the rest of the special needs policy deals with how those educational needs can be met in accordance with the legislation and resources. Children so identified will know who they are, and so will their peers, but the identification will be for educational purposes and will be recognised as such.

In general, the best guidelines may be to try to find ways of describing the special needs in terms which are as emotionally neutral as possible and are related as much as possible to the particular difficulties children have in doing particular things, rather than trying to relate the definition to the child itself. The policy should be based on an identification of children with special needs in terms of:

- what teaching methods do they need to achieve certain educational tasks;
- emotionally neutral statements;
- being consistent with the general values expressed by school of helping children learn;
- avoiding patronising the child by making the assumption that they will always be dependent to some degree (which can also have a disastrous effect on motivation);
- creating as little implication as possible for other areas of the child's life.

These forms are already capable of being applied from time to time to the full 16 per cent with minor or temporary special needs, as well as the 2 per cent with more serious and long-lasting needs. Through the very frequency of use such means of definition will become that much less remarkable.

The precise nature of the definition of special needs used in a school also has implications for the child's self-image. Most children know all too well when they have difficulty learning things, whether relating to the academic content or social relationships and behaviour. It is clearly a help when others recognise that they have a difficulty and assist them to make progress. It is much more counter-productive if the school's process of identifying children stops at the identification phase, because that may only give both teachers and the children themselves a reason for early lack of achievement in the given task. The whole point of education after all is to promote achievement, not to justify the lack of it.

## The Role of Academic Achievement in Social Values of the School

Academic attainment is one of the primary tasks of all schools. Since the 1988 Education Act, and with the continued insistence on management by performance indicators and formula budgets, academic achievements have if anything increased in their importance for schools. This scale of values however needs to be transformed for it to provide effective motivation and a sense of relevance for children with special needs. Almost all teachers are familiar with this dilemma, but reaching a consensus across staff as to how children with special needs can be encouraged to remain involved with educational tasks relevant for them is a major question. Many schools attempt to recognise effort as well as achievement in the Annual Report to parents, and this is clearly a step in the right direction. Some schools have attempted to provide school related tasks for pupils at all attainment ranges, so as to give all children who wish to some opportunity for doing tasks which gain recognition from the whole school community. Foster and Thompson (1991) gives some further examples of this, but the general principles are well known to many teachers.

## Equal or Special ?

This is another familiar dilemma well known to teachers involved with pupils with special needs. Should the responsibility of the school system be limited to ensuring that all pupils are treated equally, or should pupils with special needs be given extra consideration and help in meeting their educational and social targets? Many teachers managing a class feel instinctively that they have to operate on the basis of identical expectations in terms of behaviour for everyone yet are uncomfortably aware that in fact they are more involved with some children than with others in their group. These may be the children who make the most demands, they may be those children who sit near the front of the class, they may be the boys rather than the girls. Children with special needs can easily cause tensions in class for the teachers, because teachers know they need attention and help yet often feel unable to provide enough of it. The whole school behaviour policy will need to clarify these expectations for teachers, and convey the idea to children that they are not all identical, and that sometimes teacher attention is properly given on a basis of need, not time equivalence. To achieve 'equality of opportunity' it may be necessary to give some pupils more time than others for short periods of time.

*Inclusion in Social Groups in School*

Most schools have a number of semi-formal social groups, supported by staff, which children can become involved with should they wish, and should their interests and aptitudes match the needs of the activity. These can range from chess clubs to sport teams and from local field trips to foreign skiing trips. Does the relative lack of attainment by the children with special needs mean that they are less likely to be included in such activities? Can the activities be so designed as to permit them to participate?

All these issues give answers to the central question for the school, which each school answers in its own way. That is just what is the responsibility that the school community has towards those with special needs amongst them? When the general principles have been restated, what do they mean in practice? The 1993 Act gives a legal statement, which remains at the level of generality, that the school governors should use their best endeavours to ensure that the children's needs are known and that provision is made to meet those needs. A whole school behaviour policy to clarify expectations and practices to encourage children with special needs to make the best of their years of schooling will come to be recognised as an important part of the school's provision.

## Important elements of a whole school behaviour policy for inclusive education

After clarifying some of these basic principles in their own mind, the whole school policy project management group will need to consider what the full range of whole school behaviour policies for inclusive education might mean. For anti-bullying and anti-racist policies, the main requirement is that the school should encourage the children through all means possible to relate constructively with one another and to minimise aggression and violence. With policies for inclusive education the school has a more specific responsibility, that is to actively promote the educational achievement of those children with special needs, as well as minimising tensions arising in a way similar to those responsibilities in the other two areas. This extra responsibility means that a policy which encourages inclusive education by influencing the behaviour amongst children and between adults and children is part of a larger special needs policy, directed to the identification of children with special needs and making successful provision for them. When discussing the behavioural inclusive education policies, there will be a number of points where there will be some overlap with the more general special needs policies of the school. In this discussion, the main focus will be the behavioural policies.

To be effective, the behavioural policy for inclusive education needs to deal with:

1. Awareness raising that disability exists outside the school and within it, and that experience of disability for the person concerned is often an experience of frustration, placing extra difficulties on trying to achieve, and partial marginalisation by many groups.
2. Awareness of the range of disabilities that people may experience, from emotional pressures, specific medical conditions such as poor hearing, speech difficulties, epilepsy, and forms of difficulty in learning. This area also needs to stress the difference between having a handicap and having a disability – that many of us experience some handicapping conditions, even in a mild form but that given effort and determination on the part of the person concerned and some understanding and support from the people around them, these handicaps can be minimised and need not turn into disabilities.
3. Making the social justice argument that non-disabled people should not use differences in ability or attainment as reasons for rejection or exploitation.
4. That for the same reasons, institutional practices should not be so designed that they in effect do discriminate against people with disabilities.
5. That this question of institutional discrimination can be asked in a more precise way through enquiring whether people with some degree of disability can become members of the various group activities that the institution promotes.

As with policies in the other two areas, the detailing and implementation of policies in this inclusive education area would need to go through the same phases of awareness raising, consultation, and communication of the policy once defined. Special needs behaviour policies may pose slightly more of a challenge to the existing procedures in school, in that obviously the school staff and the management team would need to examine their current practice prior to the whole school discussion of policy, in order to avoid any too glaringly obvious examples of current school practice ignoring such principles.

*Delivering Whole School Behaviour Policies for Inclusive Education Through the Curriculum*

The general principles of delivery through the curriculum are similar to the procedures for the other two policy areas. As before, both the pastoral curriculum and the mainstream subject areas can be involved, with some co-ordination across these. Again the same general structure of curriculum audit might apply, to clarify a core group of concepts and ideas and skills through the pastoral curriculum, and then for subject specialists to identify places where these basic concepts can be elaborated in the mainstream subject areas. A good outline of the overall 'disability awareness' curriculum is presented by Galloway (1989), where he separates the area into concepts, facts, attitudes, and skills. Under 'concepts' he includes ideas such as the effects of treatment of minor handicaps, the idea of discrimination for and against disabled people, and the functions of helping organisations. Under 'facts', he includes facts such as the range of common disabilities in a class (e.g. short-sightedness etc.), common sources of confusion for non-disabled people (e.g. perceiving people with hearing loss as if they had intellectual handicaps) and the achievements of disabled people. He gives examples of attitudes as including the fear of disability, the attitudes of major world religions to disability, and disability in literature (e.g. the figure of Long John Silver in *Treasure Island*). His list of skills include making a survey of local provision for disabled people, and making maps to give the information gathered in the survey in visual form.

Galloway also includes some useful discussion on more general aspects of personal and social education in school, as it relates to children with special needs.

An interesting account of a case study of one secondary school's attempts to foster disability awareness is provided by Quicke, Beasley, and Morrison (1991). This took the form of twinning the school with a nearby special school for children with severe learning difficulties, and including discussions on special needs issues in the curriculum of the mainstream school. Children and staff from each school visited the other school, to learn as much as possible about their partner school.

In many ways one of the new elements in a curriculum easiest to introduce is the provision of extra resource material in the form of fictional accounts of disability amongst children. Many examples will occur to teachers in the normal course of events, and in addition Quicke (1985) has produced an effective review of a large number of accounts of disability in modern children's fiction, with detailed discussion of how the different books can be used in illustrating particular themes in class such as the development of friendships across the divide, such as is vividly portrayed in the film *'The Rain Man'*, and the relationship between children and disabled adults.

# CHAPTER 5

# Social Control – Supervision, Sanctions and Environmental Design

## Supervision to minimise victimisation

When hearing of incidents of victimisation in the course of everyday life, the response of many people is just to ask *'why don't they just stop it?'*. In many people's eyes, the extent of the effort to 'just stop it' by the school staff is a fairly major indicator of their commitment to a smoothly running school. In one sense the whole operation of a whole school policy is evidence of a commitment to stopping it in as an effective way as possible, and part of a whole school policy is the attention given to providing effective supervision over those areas of a school where the incidents occur. A minority of incidents occur in class, often in the form of verbal comments or threats, and often when the class is getting settled or is moving to another room. The major places where victimisation occurs however is out of class, on the playground at break-times and lunchtimes, and in the general process of moving about the school. Schools will already have their own patterns of supervision of such areas, and as with the other elements of whole school policies the need is often not for complete application of new procedures but for review and improvement on existing ones. When the policies have been worked out and disseminated throughout the school, the behaviour which is acceptable and that which is not acceptable should be reasonably clearly understood by both staff and children. Much of the difficulty of effective supervision occurs round the boundary of acceptable behaviour, and those children who find themselves wanting to carry on being aggressive towards their classmates are adept at presenting their behaviour as inside the limits of acceptability, rather than over it. In the case of bullying particularly, the bullies have a great incentive to keep the victimisation within the limits of acceptability, as they have a longer long term interest in establishing stable patterns of victimisation.

These problems with the boundary of acceptability are crucial for effective implementation of policies, which is why the original working out of the policy has to be done in some detail. Usually, single incidents can only be taken on their own, as part of the psychological damage of patterns of victimisation occur precisely because they are repeated and targeted at the same individuals. Judgements of frequency, intensity, and intent are relevant in deciding whether a particular piece of aggressive behaviour should be treated as a part of the usual rough and tumble of play or as part of a victimisation cycle.

Definition and maintenance of the boundaries of acceptable behaviour is also crucial because they will be constantly tested, and a part of the intention of those testing the boundaries is to push back the limits, and make slightly more extreme behaviour acceptable on successive occasions.

## The Development of Patterns of Behaviour

Maintaining the limits of acceptable behaviour is also crucial because of the way which behaviour does change. Many members of the public, and some would say an appreciable minority of teachers (Philips, 1989) tend to perceive children in terms of stereotypes. A part of that stereotype is that they are likely to behave in an unacceptable manner in a variety of ways, that they are likely to reject the educational values of the school and that there is little chance of them changing. In fact, children's behaviour does develop its patterns over a period of time, either becoming more mature and responsible and showing appropriate behaviour, or as being more and more inclined to challenge the expected norms and seek to push back the limits of acceptable behaviour. A large number of children are quite capable of behaving in a generally anti-social manner in schools, or anywhere else, and if the expression of standards in schools and other institutions is sufficiently weak and sufficiently flexible for normally unacceptable behaviour to be tolerated, more and more children will behave in a less and less acceptable fashion. What in actual fact is happening when this process occurs is that the children's behaviour is becoming more and more under the influence of their own peer groups, and is directed towards the aims of that peer group rather than the aims of the school.

As well as children's behaviour changing in a way which is consistent with the expressed standards of behaviour in the groups to which they belong, the behaviour of any individual child will also change in a number of situations they encounter. For example if the child finds it possible to challenge one adult by representing the situation in such a way that another adult will join in that challenge, they are actually learning the strategy of playing one adult off against the other. Having learnt that strategy, then it's perfectly possible for them to attempt to apply that strategy in other situations. The more that strategy is successful for that child in any particular context, then the more they are likely to assume that they can manipulate situations so as to get their own way, and be less and less likely to accept the direct authority of the school staff without a fairly serious attempt to challenge it. The role of supervision in school is specifically related to social control, intended to minimise the occurrence of those forms of behaviour which do break the standards defined as acceptable by the whole school policy.

The expectation of the community for most schools is that over the years the children are in school they do learn to abide by the general social rules of the greater society, as expressed in the microcosm of society inside the school grounds. Through being given opportunities to behave responsibly and appropriately, and having some negative consequences attached to not behaving appropriately, society expects a school will turn out well behaved citizens. Economically, constant supervision has a lot of disadvantages. It is relatively expensive and often simply impossible to provide in many situations outside school. A far preferred outcome for the child is that by the age of sixteen they have established their links into positive behaviour cycles acceptable to as large a number of social groups as possible.

## Supports for the Supervision Process

One of the lessons learned from consulting children in the development of whole school anti-bullying behaviour policies and of discussing possible classroom rules with children in the pursuit of general positive behaviour policies is that the vast majority of children both accept the need for rules and principles and also actively desire them. When they are expected to feel involved with the drawing up of classroom rules and more general school behaviour policies, they actively support those policies and the implementation of them. One of the telling indices of the effectiveness of anti-bullying whole school policies is the extent to which children are prepared to tell teachers when they know of incidents of bullying. A school with no policy in place can expect to have around 20 to 30 per cent of its children informing teachers, whereas a school with a policy in place for a number of years can expect a 100 per cent response to involve teachers (Rigby and Slee, 1993, Thompson and Arora, 1991). Part of drawing up the rules is also the steps towards implementation of the rules, involving supervision and processes. One school faced with the dilemma of how to find enough responsible supervisors for certain areas of the school for certain times of the day turned to its own prefect system, both broadening that out in terms of tasks and also extending its membership (Foster and Thompson, 1991). In these particular developments, all the prefects were attached to a particular class in their junior school, two of them to each first year class, and they spent lunchtimes in the first year classrooms. Access to their classrooms with two young adults present greatly increased a sense of security of the twelve-year-olds. The scheme also led to the development of more positive relationships between the older and the younger children, giving both groups a structured understanding of their responsibilities to one another.

Further examples of students assisting their classmates at lunchtime arose from the Sheffield DfE project. In one secondary school, students established and ran a peer counselling service at lunchtime to support those students who were feeling vulnerable to discrimination and harassment (Cowie and Sharp, 1992, Sharp, Silkins and Cowie, 1994). Evaluation of the service showed that it was particularly valued by younger pupils and pupils with special educational needs. In a primary school, Year 6 pupils rotated responsibility as 'play helpers'. Their job was to initiate co-operative play activities with younger pupils and to mediate in minor disputes.

Another group of staff with a strong interest in effective supervision practices is of course the teachers. In some schools a large amount of teacher time is spent on constant response to an apparently unending series of minor irritations, often suffered in silence by the teachers concerned because of their reluctance to appear to be having any 'discipline problems'. Including the process of supervision in a whole school behaviour policy discussion and later implementation makes it easier for staff to approach the issues by sharing the frustrations, and then enables sharp enough action to be taken which actually has some effect.

## Supervisors Being There

One of the first questions in a supervision review is what areas need to be supervised at what times and by whom. The groups of people involved in the supervision are teaching staff, lunchtime supervision staff, and senior pupils, and their supervisory timetables need to be clearly stated and known. Simple punctuality can also go some way towards strengthening supervision.

## Knowing What To Do In Supervision

Knowing what to do depends on knowing what should be done, i.e. supervisors knowing the contents of the whole school policies, and being able to identify those situations in practice when action is required. Knowing what to do is greatly improved by having to play a part in the development of the policy expectations in the first place, and having been active in trying to identify the ambiguous areas where application of the policies may be difficult. Talking and thinking in public about situations met in practice, in a framework where solutions are expected, provides a good opportunity for learning. When clarity of expectations is achieved via such processes, most staff appreciate some help in learning what to do and when to do it. In many schools supervision skills are assumed to be an instinctive activity, which probationary teachers bring from their colleges with their certificates. As we discussed above, in fact supervision of children is quite a complex process involving complex social judgements about the meaning and emotional tone of children's activities, as well as responding when the blood flows. Training in supervision can either be provided by specific in-school courses involving some outside input, some 'idealised' discussions of incidents shown on videotape, and some discussion and role play of actual incidents occurring in the playground, and it could also involve the 'apprenticeship' type learning whereby more senior colleagues supervise with more junior ones alongside them. Such paired supervision also makes it possible for discussion to take place between staff when the incidents are fresh in the memory.

These discussion and training processes are relatively uncomplicated when taking place between teaching staff. They become appreciably more difficult when involving non-teaching staff such as lunchtime supervisors or senior pupils. When such other personnel are involved in supervision they tend to be involved in supervision in specific settings with specific groups of children, and it is perfectly possible to set up specific training covering those particular situations. In practice, all the teaching staff would then be seen as senior to these two other groups of non-teaching staff, and so even if their training is not undertaken at the same time it would be important for all the teachers to have undergone the same training as lunchtime supervisors and senior pupils, as a part of their own training. In that way the teaching staff will know what to expect of the two other groups, and also the two other groups will know how to relate to the teaching staff. They will know when incidents are sufficiently serious to bring to the attention of the teaching staff later, and they will have learnt something of the role of discussion in clarifying expectations of behaviour and appropriate supervisory action. They also will have learnt the idea of supervision as a process of active engagement with the children concerned, moving over the area to be supervised, looking to check on potentially difficult situations emerging, and pausing to chat briefly with groups of children to indicate presence and accessibility. Interpreted in this way, supervision can be very effective in preventing the build-up of small incidents into more major ones.

*Management of Lunchtime Supervision*

Staff employed as student supervisors can find themselves in a fairly anomalous position in the school, in that they are only involved for the central part of the day, they are paid much less than almost all other school staff, they are usually assumed to be from a different social background to many of the school staff, with much lower educational attainments themselves, and often have an ambiguous management structure in the school. Just who do they report to and what do they report about? Due to these institutional circumstances, lunchtime supervisors can often form a very isolated and undervalued group in the school community. In spite of this however they are virtually in charge of the children under relatively difficult circumstances for an extended period of time in an environment which often gives little scope for constructive activity amongst the children. One of the beneficial side effects of developing whole school behaviour policies is that the process has to include the lunchtime supervisors, who then feel their managerial links with the school strengthened and often benefit greatly from the recognition and clarification of their role which follows. It is also possible to devise local training courses for lunchtime supervisors, sometimes mounted by external agencies with some participation from the school staff, or possibly completely from within the staff resources. Managerially, the aim is then to give them persons and hierarchical links to report to, and to give them opportunities for discussion and review of their own supervisory activities, to identify any problems early on and gain staff help to overcome them. However just because they may see themselves as a very junior group in the overall school management, the procedures would need to be set up in such a way as to protect the personal identities of the supervisors. If some junior teachers are reluctant to report emerging discipline problems for fear of being seen as incompetent to some degree, so will lunchtime supervisors be reluctant to identify problems occurring if they feel that this directly weakens their individual status in the school.

Sometimes Local Education Authorities or their agencies do run lunchtime supervisor training courses (Sharp, 1993), and there are also a number of training packs available which schools can implement. In addition, some teacher journals have begun publishing discussions of the behaviour of children during lunchtime and the supervision of it (see for example, Imich and Jefferies, 1989, Blatchford and Sharp, 1993, Boulton and Smith, 1986).

## Sanctions

As with any system of expectations of appropriate behaviour, encouraged by group norms and promoted values, some of the violation of accepted standards are interpreted as 'breaking the rules'. Part of the discussion of the whole school policy includes the clarification of the points where not meeting expectations of appropriate behaviour becomes defined as breaking the rules, and in a formal institutional sense rule breaking means incurring some form of sanctions or to use a more old fashioned word 'punishments'. The word 'sanctions' generally expresses the need more accurately than punishments, which implies a more or less aggressive response to the individual breaking the rules which assumes that the student is in complete control of the behaviour concerned. When developing the whole school policies in the three behavioural areas, the same conditions apply - when certain rules are broken, then sanctions occur.

*General Aims of Sanctions in School*

School staff running the discipline system in schools would typically see the system as having multiple aims. These would usually include:

1. The ultimate aim of any sanctions system is to reduce the frequency of rule breaking, and one way of doing this is to find ways of emphasising the importance of complying with the rules.
2. Teachers would usually hope that sanctions would make re-offending less likely. Sometimes this is assumed to be due to the direct effect of the sanctions on the individual student involved, and sometimes also to be due to the so-called 'deterrent effect'.
3. Most people considering a sanctions system would want to include an element of social justice, that is some negative consequences for the offender as a direct consequence of some harm having been caused to other members of the community. This is also seen as serving the first two purposes above – to make the re-offending less likely for those who might be tempted, and to emphasise the role system itself. The precise form of negative consequences varies with the system and is not necessarily of the 'personal punitive' type that is often imagined to be.
4. In operating a sanctions system, most staff would also include the aim of avoiding having to use the sanctions so frequently that the students in general, and their frequent offenders in particular, become used to enduring the sanctions which are typically used. Too frequent use of a sanctions system also obviously adds a further administrative burden onto the people implementing it, and in addition tends to increase the alienation of those individuals falling foul of the system. A crucial element here is what other parallel positive processes are operating alongside the sanctions system. If some children only receive staff attention when they break the rules, their emotional involvement with the school system as a whole is likely to decrease fairly rapidly. Such a reaction on the part of the individual is likely to reduce the effect of the sanctions system itself, by reducing the significance for the individual of the element of social disapproval in the rule breaking. To achieve this last aim, those implementing a sanctions system use various strategies. These can range from not actively seeking to identify instances of rule breaking, through 'turning a blind eye' to the rule breaking when it is observed, as far as a more or less formal 'caution' system, where the offender is let off with a warning. These strategies may or may not be tacitly approved of by those managing the sanctions system, but they do serve this particular set of aims of those operating the system. The aims themselves are legitimate, but the methods of achieving the aims may on occasions tend to weaken the value system on which the expectations of appropriate behaviour are based. One of the methods sometimes used in situations where breaking of certain rules are very frequent, is to

approach the situation on a planned incremental basis. This implies that the overall period during which improved rule observation is planned for is broken into several phases. In the earlier phases only the more extreme examples of rule breaking automatically attract sanctions, and when the number of such incidents have reduced, then in phase two sanctions are extended down a scale into more minor areas. In this way the sanctions system can be applied consistently, and so be effective, but at the same time does not produce an impossibly large number of incidents where it needs to be used and staff are not seen to be colluding with the rule breakers by only 'noticing' a small proportion of the actual rule breaking which occurs.

As these aims usually form the basis of the existing sanctions system in 'school, they will be the same general aims relevant for the sanctions used when rules in whole school behaviour policies are broken. The policies themselves should both help define for the school staff just when a certain kind of behaviour is seen to be serious enough to trigger the sanctions system, and also to give the teachers the school's support in implementing that sanctions system. By defining the offences clearly, the policy also serves to increase compliance with the expectations of appropriate behaviour by clarifying them for the pupils.

All schools have evolved their own sanctions system, dependent on the school's history. The actual sanctions used typically include the following general categories:

1. Explicit teacher disapproval. This can either take the form of the formal warning mentioned above, or it can be a more informal reaction from the teacher to incidents related to forgetfulness, general pressure of events, or when the incidents involve a particular student who is not usually involved in intentional rule breaking. The strength of such formal and informal warnings gains a large element of its effectiveness from the relationship between the student breaking the rules and the person expressing the disapproval. If the disapproving adult has a relatively high social status and on other occasions has a positive relationship with the offender, the expression of disapproval is more likely to be effective than when those conditions do not apply. The effectiveness is also helped if the offender themselves can recognise the rule breaking as such, and realises that they have transgressed standards generally accepted by the group concerned. In incidents where the adult's rule enforcer has a low status in the eyes of the offender, where disapproval has been expressed often before, and where the offender does not accept that the particular rule concerned has any wider social support, the disapproval is almost certain to be at least totally ineffective and at worst likely to actively increase the degree of rejection which the offender

feels for the legitimacy of the rule concerned and for the person expressing disapproval.

2. Informal and formal warnings are usually the first steps in the sanctions
system. The second step is often restitution, where the offender is
instructed to do something which demonstrates acceptance after incidents such as knocking a pile of exercise books onto the floor the
offender is told to pick them all up again and put them in alphabetical
order. This kind of restitutional sanctions can easily be extended to
make a bigger impact by, in the example given above, extending the
sanctions to include tidying up all the rest of the shelf of books as well.

3. Most schools still have some kind of detention system, a general depri-
vation of personal time.

4. Most secondary schools use some kind of 'report' system, whereby if
particular individuals do develop habits of behaving anti-socially in a
number of different lessons, after the initial sanctions the pupil is
instructed to report to the class teacher at the end of each class to certi-
fy their good behaviour during that class period. This system has the
advantage of putting the class teachers and the offenders into some kind
of contact, and allowing the class teachers space to formally acknow
ledge efforts on the part of the student to behave properly. In addition of
course it demonstrates the width of the school's concern to the individual concerned.

5. A further general sanction is to involve other, more high status adults in
the processes of expressing disapproval. Inside school, these are usually more senior teaching staff, but one source of extra pressure on almost
all students which they do dislike intensely is when the school involves
the parents and invites their parents to express disapproval as well at
home. In surveys of children's attitudes to different kinds of sanctions,
the sanction of involving parents is usually the one that they consider
most objectionable and the one they would do most to avoid.

All sanctions of course have major limitations in that they only 'work' if
I the potential offender considers themselves highly likely to be picked up
if they do break the rules, if the offender does have some positive relationships with the institution and so is sensitive to general disapproval, and
when the rule breaking is related to behaviour which the student can control. If the student is convinced it is possible to avoid detection, the sanctions system loses its deterrent effect completely, and if the student has no
positive experiences in the institution and cares nothing for the disapproval
of the adults involved, the sanctions are unlikely to change their behaviour
in the future. If the student is unable to control their own behaviour in certain social contexts, then at the very least application of a sanction needs to
be accompanied with some analysis of the situation with the student concerned in order to assist the student to control the behaviour in the future.

In all discussions of the effects of sanctions, staff need to bear in mind that most children's behaviour will only change gradually over time – they will 'offend' less and less frequently for a period before they stop completely. If this frequency reduction is not happening, sanctions are not working.

*Important Strengths of the Sanctions System for Whole School Behaviour Policies*

Most of the elements of the typical school discipline system described above are relevant for instances of rule breaking in the whole school behaviour policy area. However three particular aspects stand out as being central to effective sanctions in the implementation of whole school behaviour policies. These are the need to reduce the extent to which teachers express direct aggression when implementing sanctions, the need to increase the contact between the offender and the victims in a controlled situation, and early parental involvement.

The need to reduce the direct aggression expressed by teachers arises because the basic mechanisms of racism and bullying, and to a lesser extent discrimination against special needs pupils, lies with the general assumption that using aggression in the course of everyday social life is perfectly acceptable to the wider community. Sanctions may reduce the incidence of racism and bullying in schools where the supervision is effective and most of the occasions are noticed, but longer term prevention needs a re-statement of the general social value that aggression is not acceptable. If the school staff find themselves using aggression towards the children when implementing sanctions, they are unwittingly encouraging their belief that aggression is acceptable. Additionally of course using aggression with offenders, especially on repeated occasions, has the undesirable side effect of increasing the alienation of the children from the adult system in the school and making many of the other types of sanctions less effective.

Sanctions which increase the positive contact between the offenders and the victims have again long term preventative advantages, in that the increased contact makes it more possible that the tensions between the children can be reduced through less aggressive interactions in the future. For this to occur of course the participants concerned have to be placed in situations where they have to interact in non-aggressive ways.

The third element which is useful is that of parental involvement. Disapproval from parents is often more effective than disapproval from teaching staff in providing a negative sanction for children's behaviour, and in the situations where relatively serious aggressive incidents are occurring the stronger the disapproval expressed, the better. Where whole school behaviour policies have been worked out so as to include parents in the consultation and dissemination stages, then the involvement of parents at the point of application of sanctions is perfectly natural.

Applying these three principles to the list of actual typical classes of sanctions used in schools and described above – sanctions based on restitution, extra pressure from significant adults, and being 'on report' – would be likely to be more effective than sanctions based on the limitation of liberty or teacher disapproval. This last sanction is tricky because of the difficulty many staff find of expressing disapproval without also expressing aggression as well. Teacher disapproval when implementing sanctions in the whole school behaviour policy area are only likely to be effective if the teacher concerned has already got a strong positive relationship with the offender which has been developed in some other aspect of school life. Teacher disapproval can also have some effect if it can be broadened out and linked in with general pupil based disapproval of the same event. This is probably quite difficult to achieve at the point of implementing sanctions, and if the attempt to elicit disapproval from other children fails then attempting to implement the sanction at all has probably been counter-productive.

### Specific Kinds of Sanctions Procedures for Anti-bullying Policies

Using non-violent sanctions when incidents of bullying occur has been discussed in detail in Foster and Thompson (1991). The sanctions system in operation in this particular school at that time was based on a number of principles covering implementing sanctions for:
- relatively 'minor' harassments such as taking a pencil from some one and breaking it;
- for bullying-type name calling;
- for more traumatic major incidents.

For the minor incidents, sanctions were either restitution or specific teacher disapproval which was non-aggressive but which occupied the bully's time. For more major incidents, senior members of the school staff were automatically involved, along with a class teacher, thus emphasising the seriousness of the incident in the eyes of the school. Time was taken to establish precisely what had occurred if the incident had not been observed by supervisors, and who was directly involved and who was also acting as bystanders in the area at the time. The two members of staff would then use general group work discussion techniques involving the bully, the bystander, and the victim to establish the basic unreasonableness of the behaviour and to lead the children to suggest restitution on the part of the bully. Applied in this way, the sanctions system can be seen as a means of re-establishing relationships between the bully, the bystanders and the victim, rather than the teachers in school applying a sanctions system unilaterally which the bullies can then feel resentment about. At the end of such a discussion, a contract is made between the children whereby after they leave the room the victim clearly understands that if anything else happens they can talk about it. Frequently the bystanders who are also present in the discussion can be given the responsibility for monitoring the situation, as friends and acquaintances of the main protagonists. The aim is to specifically stress to the bystanders the need for them to prevent any future bullying getting out of hand either by reminding the protagonist directly or by informing teaching staff. The whole discussion is focussed around talking about a situation which has arisen from tension between the pupils and how to put it right. The discussion becomes a reaffirmation of those same standards of acceptable behaviour discussed in detail in the drawing up of the whole school policy. Parents were also usually involved, each set of parents being seen separately with their own child. Again parts of the aims of this meeting were to discuss the positive things that might happen at home that might help their sons or daughters not to get into these situations again. This also serves to emphasise to the student in the school that when incidents occur of any degree of seriousness, both sets of parents are inevitably informed and involved in the actions taken as a part of the general sanctions system. However, it is important that if these principles are established, then the necessary actions must be carried out by the school staff when incidents occur.

A second set of procedures which has been found to be of some effectiveness in preventing children who bully from repeating their behaviour is that developed by Pikas (1989). This was described as the 'shared concern methods' for the treatment of bullies, because it relies on stating and establishing a shared concern between the adult supervisor and the bully that the bullied pupil is unhappy about the current situation. The student doing the bullying is expected to help in some way. The procedure is based on the adult having fairly brief (10 to 15 minutes) discussions individually with both the major bully and the supporters, separately, conducted in such a way that the children concerned have no chance to communicate with each other until the end of the whole cycle of interviews with them all. The prime bully is interviewed first. No specific attempt is made to induce the bully to admit liability for the victim's emotional stress, the aim being to encourage the bully to perceive and acknowledge the negative effect on the victim and ways that this might be prevented.

Again, at the end of each interview the adult makes an explicit contract with the offender that the situation will be reviewed in some way, and that the actions of the offender are important in a successful outcome for that review, in a relatively short period of time. Experiences in the schools which have used the methods seem to indicate that it does indeed have a short term effect on the incidence of bullying, but that for long term effectiveness the monitoring processes built into the procedure have to be taken seriously (Smith and Sharp, 1994). Further details of the procedure are given in a useful collection of detailed descriptions of various interventions to reduce bullying (Sharp and Smith, 1994). It is quite helpful when applying Pikas' method of concem as a anti-bullying sanction that the staff doing so have had some training in precisely what to do in the interview with the offender. The technique is generally not difficult to learn, based on a strict sequence of four or five questions to the offender, and establishing the follow-up contract. In principle, these methods or slight variations of them should be applicable to handling incidents which involve both racism and discrimination against special needs children where those incidents follow a general bullying pattern, that is of a great imbalance of power between the bully and the victim, support for the bully by members of the bully's peer group, relative isolation of the victim, and a pattern of incidents emerging over a period of time. Discrimination against children with special needs will follow this pattern fairly frequently, and incidents of racism may follow this pattern where the victim does not have a support group of their own and is relatively isolated in the school.

## Changes to the playground environment

In recent years some schools have been increasingly recognising that many school playgrounds are actually very ill-adapted for encouraging children to play together. Systematic accounts of problems with the playground have been presented by Blatchford (1989), the DES (1990), and Ross and Ryan (1989). In general, the deficiencies in many playgrounds have been evident to a number of schools over a number of years, and some schools in all parts of the country have taken initiatives in small projects like establishing weatherproof seating areas in parts of their playgrounds for the past twenty years at least.

When concerns grow about the incidence of bullying in schools, one of the early findings was that well over half of the incidents seemed to occur in the playground, when children's activity was at its freest and only relatively lightly supervised. Improvements in playgrounds was one of the major interventions carried out by some schools in association with a whole school policy during the Sheffield DfE anti-bullying Study (Smith and Sharp, 1994). The playground based interventions were in fact one of the most popular interventions with the primary schools, and a number of the schools both initiated playground design schemes and established a 'games box' where children could take balls, bean bags, hoops and other light play equipment into the playground at break-times to encourage cooperative play.

The main problem with playgrounds arises because the wide stretches of tarmac do permit large group games such as football to be played relatively easily, but give precious little encouragement for games other than those involving chasing of some description. For maximum educational and social use, playgrounds need to provide the opportunities for children to play together in a much more diverse set of ways, and specifically to play together in ways which do not involve running around. Social play is specifically stimulated by having equipment and facilities which encourage children to play co-operatively together in groups of various sizes, where relatively small groups of two or three maybe among the most significant for children who are relatively isolated from the main peer groups in the school and who would be likely to become targets for victimisation of various sorts. The starting point for a certain amount of playground redesign is usually recognition of the problem through some concerned adults, either members of school staff or parents, and a project being set up from that to decide what to do, to find the resources to do it with, and to implement the programme.

## Managing a playground improvement scheme

A playground improvement project is distinctive enough from the development of whole school behaviour policies for it to be managed by a different project team, provided there is some overlap of membership between this project team and the main whole school policy management group. The two teams would also find it possibly useful to know when each other was planning various activities, such as consultation activities with the pupils. It is probably simpler for the students if the consultation activities are kept separate, as they have quite enough meat in themselves as separate activities rather than attempting to combine them into one. In a similar way to establishing a whole school behaviour policy, playground improvement schemes can gain a lot by having a clear consultation stage near the beginning of the project, when staff, lunchtime supervisors, parents, and particularly the children have chance to express their views on problems with playing outdoors under the current arrangements and suggestions as to how the problems might be solved. One of the advantages of a playground improvement scheme is that it gives many opportunities for work related to the main curriculum, with a need for the improvements to be detailed on maps drawn to scale, agreed plans resulting from discussions between groups of children, and communication of these ideas to groups of people such as parents and other voluntary helpers. Such communication could be in the form of reports for PTAs, or preparations for a fund raising campaign where the children can begin to think through the problems of communicating with people outside school. The specific nature of the work will clearly depend on the age of the children.

When information and ideas have been gathered in and the project team has been able to identify various aspects of a playground improvement scheme, these various aspects can be prioritised into improvement schemes achievable in the near future with currently identifiable resources, and the more ambitious schemes for which some external funding may be necessary which would only happen some months or years into the future. It is a considerable advantage that the children, parents and staff can see some of the results of their involvement fairly early on. This provides a base of motivation for the more long term aspects of the project.

One key aim is to increase the diversity of activities which are actually encouraged by the playground design and equipment. If the early data search included some direct observation of what children actually did in the playgrounds it would become evident that there are a wide range of social activities which the design could potentially support. One of the most useful ways of thinking about the playground area is in terms of various 'zones' of the playground which could be used for some of the commoner purposes. For example, the area where active ball games such as football can be played could be clearly identified, leaving space for an area to be used for small games using light portable equipment such as hoops and bean bags. Hopscotch and marbles can also be helped by having specific areas. A further major need of most playgrounds is for seating, this can often be incorporated with some of the boundary edges to the playground. In school grounds where there is some area of earth and plants, then the whole 'nature study' set of activities becomes possible, involving more ambitious projects such as pond digging and plant growing. These would need to be linked in fairly clearly with the main school curriculum and the specific subject areas with staff who are interested in using such facilities as a part of their teaching. One of the great advantages of playground improvement projects of this nature is that they attract much early approval from all concerned, and also need the same kind of consultation and decision making systems that the whole school behaviour policy implementation need (Humphries, 1994). Along with the anti-bullying policy, they provide an obvious example of areas for change where the need and the benefits are very clear. Taken as a single project, playground improvement is much less complicated than introduction of whole school behaviour policies, and so might prove a useful initial project for schools to commit themselves to, from whence they could progress to establishing whole school behaviour policies in subsequent years building on the foundation of expectations of consultation and involvement of parents that were first initiated for the playground improvement schemes. As with the establishment of whole school behaviour policies there are external sources of support that maybe available. These might include the landscape sections of local further education and higher education colleges, staff and students from arts schools in the area who might be interested in environmental art, and of course members of the parent's groups with specific skills. Considerably more detailed information and procedures is easily available from those sources cited above, and in addition Higgins (1994) gives a detailed description of the process and possibilities for efficient running of a playground improvement scheme.

# CHAPTER 6

# *Staff Development*

## Policy implementation

Policy development and implementation are a form of organisation development. If the policy is implemented effectively the ways that the organisation operates will be changed. In a sense, the whole point of 'whole school' policies is that all or most members of the school staff and pupils have made some contribution to the definition of the policies. Everyone is in a position to have different expectations of each other and to change their behaviour to each other in certain directions. The awareness raising and consultation processes early on validate the expectation of changed behaviour.

So far so good. Unfortunately, intellectual knowledge of how things ought to change and expectations that they should change is often not sufficient to actually enable people to change their behaviour. Whilst understanding and expectations may change quickly, as they are intellectual processes, behaviour changes are much slower and are achieved by a series of incremental steps which must be continually encouraged, at least in the early stages. It is usually not only the children who need to change their behaviour for effective policy implementation, but staff will need to do so as well in certain minor but significant ways. The ways they need to alter their practice covers both the curricular areas, the supervision areas, and also the form of their own emotional reactions. They will need to react more strongly to some things and more slowly to others, will need to act on a slightly different criteria than before, and will need to react with a greater appreciation of the individual needs of the particular pupil with whom they are involved.

One key area that some school staff need to develop their expertise and confidence in is the area of emotionally based communication with children. This best occurs as a slight extension of whatever skills they have in this area previously. Those teachers used to a didactic approach can extend their skills into group discussion based activities, those who are comfortable already with discussion based activities can extend further into group work involving simulations and projects, sometimes including aspects of drama and role play. Those who are fairly familiar with active tutorial work will probably possess these skills already, and may want to move on to what might best be described as counselling work with children, in that they become more able to tolerate and be supportive for children expressing their fears and worries in individual discussions with the staff member. Schools are busy places, and it is easy to let the urgency of the routine activities for both staff and students, but particularly for staff, wipe out the time for relaxed communication necessary for a child to express some of their deeper worries.

All these possible directions of development involve school staff being better able to create the conditions where children feel they can communicate safely and can expect to do so and receive some kind of support. Any forms of discrimination are highly emotionally charged, particularly for the victims, and the key competency for the teachers is to encourage children to communicate their emotional needs with them and with each other.

These competencies do not only involve communication between staff and children. Those on the project management group may well need to extend their skills of encouraging participation from individuals and groups in distant corners of the school, in allowing people to express their emotional reactions to the issues and at the same time to create enough consensus of agreement for the next steps to be taken. Skills at managing meetings are crucial, as agendas need to be set clearly so that the process of consultation, policy decision, and implementation spreads evenly across the school. Information from consultative meetings needs to be summarised and fed back to the core planning group in such a way that the particular details from different sectors of the school community are not lost in the averaging, but the feedback is appropriately structured and of appropriate length so that the co-ordinating group can relate to it easily.

During all this emergence of new skills and knowledge, the old distinction between training that benefits the individual staff member and their particular needs and aspirations on the one hand and training that benefits the school on the other will undoubtedly emerge. How important is expertise in this area for significant promotions in school, possibly as opposed to developing skills in such school activities as curriculum development, budgeting, or staff appraisal? Questions like these will certainly occur in the minds of the more junior staff who may or may not become committed to the implementation of the whole school behaviour policies, and need to be answered as clearly and honestly as possible. Certainly the range of issues in policy implementation is large enough to satisfy staff with less interest in the 'pastoral and special needs' areas, but these may need to be pointed out specifically for the person concerned. Implementation of the policy can use people whose skills are developing in almost any area, and who feel they have some commitment to give.

## Staff development and the climate of supported change

Introduction of whole school policies is an example of organisational change, needing to have roots in changes seen as a useful and necessary response to external conditions and the results of internal quality monitoring, rather than as essentially a threat to the status quo both for individual staff members and for groups. Creating this climate is a long term job for any manager, and focuses around creating an environment which is genuinely supportive of individuals as they change and creating a general atmosphere of trust in the professionalism and social justice of the school systems

### *The Social Psychology of Individual Staff Development*

Over the last few years a number of researchers have been interested in teachers' responses to the need for change and their responses to problems encountered in the workplace. One of the earlier studies was by Wagner (1987), who was interested in the ways that teachers thought about some of the problems they encountered. She explored both the method of thinking about the problems and what issues were seen as constituting problems in school. From detailed interview analysis, she came to the conclusion that one frequently occurring pattern in teachers' thinking was a form of circular argument which essentially got nowhere, because the teachers posed questions without making attempts to systematically resolve them. They moved from one issue to another before coming to any conclusions on the first, and considered strategies and goals in the abstract without ever actually trying to put them into practice. Teachers seemed to be either reluctant or incapable of recognising the inappropriateness of these particular circular inconclusive patterns of analysis, which Wagner called 'knots'. She felt that these circular arguments were often associated with strong emotional components such as anxiety or attachment. When she looked at the topics which were most associated with the circular arguments, the topic which generated the most knots was that of 'fellow teachers'. This was much more significant than issues of lesson content or even of problems of discipline and control. If an appreciable number of teachers feel that their fellow teachers are significant sources of problems rather than support, it becomes easy to see why processes of staff development and positive response to change are sometimes difficult to establish in schools. This picture of some teachers seeing their colleagues as representing problem areas rather than support is also paralleled in other studies. Little (1990) reviewed a large number of American studies of teacher interaction with their colleagues and came to the conclusion that the studies generally gave a picture of relative professional isolation amongst experienced teachers, with the few examples of genuine support and joint effort providing relatively rare exceptions to this general conclusion. Little is not claiming that teachers in the research reviewed by her did not enjoy the social company of their colleagues but that those colleagues did not provide any support or stimulation for their professional development. Lieberman and Miller (1990), in a paper in the same volume, came to the conclusion that part of the reason for this relative secrecy over professional matters was that even though teachers lost possible sources of support and encouragement, they also gained the security of not having to face their failures publicly. Lortie (1975) considered that parts of teachers' reluctance to consult colleagues over professional matters was that they looked for their primary reward as positive interactions and feedback from their pupils. This was also the conclusion which arose from, a more recent study into sources of teacher satisfaction (Poppleton, 1989).

To whom do teachers turn for their reference groups then, to provide social validation for their practice? Jennifer Nias (1985) specifically looked at this question, interviewing teachers who had been teaching between two and nine years. One of the more surprising findings from this study was that many teachers only needed a very small reference group, often only one other person who could be either a colleague in the school, a head teacher or other member of the senior staff, or even a visiting professional. The amount of support gained by the teacher from such individuals seemed to be much greater than would be expected, both in terms of the minimal time spent in communication between the teacher and her reference group and the very small size of that reference group itself. In addition, the majority of teachers in the study said that there had been some points during their careers when they had no adult reference group in school at all. If this happened then they sought it in attending outside courses or from talking to 'like minded' friends.

Nias also came to the conclusion that teachers constructed their self concept as teachers inside school only through conversations with those few people in their own reference groups, which were not at all representative of the generality of colleagues in school. She thought that this was because teachers actually shared constructs about the teaching process and children with their reference groups. If they attempted to discover what constructs they shared with the other colleagues, the expected lack of support for these particular ideas would be likely to be destructive of the sense of self of the teacher rather than supportive. She felt that this line of reasoning was some explanation of why teachers seem to actively avoid talking about important basic aspects of work with the generality of their colleagues. She did identify a counter process however when teachers felt under threat from pupils, and then sought out colleagues for general social support. Colleagues could provide this social support quite adequately entering into what Nias called a 'false consensus' in the staff room, where support was given in a very general way and detailed discussions about teaching practices was still avoided. Back in the classroom, the teacher continued to teach in a way which was consistent with their own self image and also consistent with their earlier teaching practices. Some of this work is summarised by Miller (1994), who was interested in examining particular situations where teachers had in fact changed their practice to deal with difficult pupils but who had kept this change in practice to themselves. They were quite reluctant to even inform other colleagues of their relative success with particular pupils following such a change in practice. He saw this resistance to even share positive change as related to a reluctance to challenge or seek any change in the existing 'false consensus' between staff, particularly as it applied to particular pupils.

Research such as this clearly indicates some of the unspoken barriers to developing effective collaboration between teaching staff members when designing and implementing whole school behaviour policies. These findings also reinforce the general need for staff development round the whole school behaviour policy issues to encourage staff to discuss fairly emotionally loaded issues to do with the relationship between them and the children in their class in as supportive a way as possible, with a specific end in view which is advantageous to all concerned. In some ways, the language of the dynamics of bullying and other conflict laden situations in school may begin to provide a common language for colleagues to use to communicate together with. The basic concepts as outlined in chapter 2 are not difficult, and would already be found in most teachers' understanding of children. The need may not be to introduce these concepts to teachers, but to focus their use of them through orderly agendas and discussion processes.

Bearing these general problems in mind, it is then possible to move on to the more or less standard staff development processes in school, in this instance clearly focused on the general needs for knowledge and skill related both to teaching and supervising groups of children which include some who can behave as aggressors in certain circumstances and some who end up victims. In addition, staff also need the understanding of the nature of a whole school process and how to play their part in both designing and implementing it. In both these areas, the staff will find it easier to learn the new ideas than to learn to behave in new ways, but the changes in behaviour that they will need to learn are almost always only slight extensions of their current teaching skills. There will already be a certain proportion of individuals in school with the necessary skills to implement the policy, both in terms of their interactions with children and in terms of the dynamics of implementation of the policy itself. These existing skills need recognition, and social validation from the management by public acknowledgement in some way. Such acknowledgement need not necessarily be completely individually based – groups of people, for example year tutors, could be involved with policy development in specific ways

90

and that public responsibility would in itself be an acknowledgement of existing skills. Not all staff members will support and implement the policy one hundred per cent anyway, but those who find change in themselves in the required directions particularly difficult should be in a relatively small minority and should understand enough of the overall policy not to actively attempt to sabotage its development. If there are any such individuals in school, it is likely that the more they feel threatened by the new developments the more their resistance will harden. It is important, therefore, to avoid these individuals feeling threatened if at all possible.

## In-Service education for whole school behaviour policy development

The research quoted above gives a somewhat pessimistic picture of what may be happening to members of school staffs in their search for support and professional development. In the light of this, effective in-service education will need to set up a common concern which school staffs can appreciate is relevant to them and will help them teach in the way they would ideally like to. To achieve this, a clear generally supported theme has to be put forward, a common language of facts, concepts, and purposes has to be established, in a general climate of recognition of a need for change. Whole school behaviour policy development, especially as regards an anti-bullying policy, gives a good theme which meets all of these criteria in most schools. Implementing the staff development process round such areas needs a clear understanding of the school focussed model of in-service education, consultation to define the particular needs that the particular staff members have, a certain amount of organisation of training events and processes, and some evaluation and review of the training processes when staff have had a chance to put the ideas and methods into practice.

## School focussed in-service education and training

Whole school behaviour policy development requires the active involvement of a large proportion of school staff, and also needs to operate in an environment where staff generally support each other in structuring the patterns of relationships between themselves and the children in school. The obvious model of in-service development which has these characteristics is the school focussed in-service model, with some degree of support from external consultants. The approach is very well described in detail by Nixon (1989) who provides a concise, readable, and precise set of methods for consultation with the staff and methods for the delivery of in-service training. This particular volume is in fact the introduction to the 'Inset Workshops for Schools' series, published by Macmillan Education. Three of these sets of workshop materials are concerned with health and sex education, multi-cultural education, and equal opportunities policy on gender, and so give a very good set of examples of workshops for developing whole school policies which can easily be extended to relate to anti-bullying, and inclusive education behaviour policies. In the immediately following sections we will illustrate the application of the methods discussed by Nixon and the authors of the workshop materials into the areas of the anti-bullying policy development.

*Knowledge and Skills Needed for Implementation of Anti-bullying Policy*

For successful implementation of the policy school staff need to have information about the nature of bullying, to find out the extent of bullying in their own school, and to develop their skills in handling children in the various preventative and social control processes described earlier. They also need to learn to evaluate and review the extent of the change in bullying, and to understand and participate in the overall in-school management processes by which the policy is constructed and sustained. In practice, a number of staff in school will possess these skills, or an appreciable proportion of these skills already, and a major part of the in-service education planning process is to establish in which particular areas the staff do need support. External consultants can often be of considerable help in modelling the processes of assessing the incidence of bullying, helping staff plan surveys and other methods of establishing how much bullying occurs and in the process teaching them the skills of implementing the surveys themselves.

This process of establishing detailed needs inside a general area is described very well by Nixon (1989 p.28). He describes a questionnaire-based needs survey, with two stages. The first stage seeks general information on what areas of information and skills individual staff members feel they need training in, by providing a list of types of information and specific skills which informants can choose. After the information from this survey has been analysed, Nixon recommends using a much smaller forced choice questionnaire to establish staff preferences for particular composite training events. If this model was used to assess training needs for implementing an anti-bullying policy, questions in the 'information' section might include:

- how is bullying to be defined in school?
- how can its incidence be generally assessed?
- how much bullying is there in this school compared with other schools?
- among which age groups and classes is the bullying most marked?
- in which areas of the school does bullying tend to occur most?
- why does bullying occur?
- what happens if nothing is done about it?
- how should the normal sanction system of the school be used?

● what is the best way of involving parents?

When the replies to surveys of this type are analysed, it will be clear that the information requested has to be provided in different ways. Some questions can be answered by straight information-giving sessions using external consultants, answers to some will only be apparent as the anti-bullying policy goes into effect. The early training procedures however can identify those areas of information where it is possible to provide specific relevant information, at the outset, and those which have to be agreed on in the various consultation stages in developing the policy itself.

In a similar way the project management group can identify the particular skills most needed by staff members. In this case, the needs survey questionnaire 'skills' section would include such possibilities as:

● skills in counselling victims of bullying;
● skills in group work to use in form tutor periods;
● skills in using Pikas' method of Common Concern when working with bullies;
● skills in discussing the behaviour of bullies with them and their parents;
● using surveys to assess the extent of bullying in school;
● managing a policy review meeting for one year group;
● identifying which incidents involving aggression between children-should be treated as bullying and which ones should not;
● (for senior or more experienced staff) skills in working with junior staff in meetings with parents so as to develop their skills.

In the same way as for the needs for information, when these results are analysed it is possible to describe a small number of more general areas which staff can be invited to choose between in a forced choice survey. It is clearly impossible to meet everyone's staff development needs exactly in any group based training situation, but through consultation such as this school staff can be involved in a process of defining the content of the training sessions and appropriate methods of delivery to make the training as relevant and as effective as possible.

**Organising in-service training events**

From a needs survey such as that above, the project management group can begin to identify possible training events which meet the needs of the staff. These may take various forms. As discussed above, one part of the needs for information can be met through the consultation processes in designing the policy. These areas can be immediately removed from the general 'training' needs, the consultation procedures for the policy having been checked to ensure that they are sufficiently structured to provide answers to these questions. The remaining needs will be met from a mixture of joint workshops on information or skills development on fairly specific topics, possibly involving staff from other neighbouring schools and which may or may not involve outside consultants as trainers; in school processes, where the skills needed are specific to the particular procedures in the school concerned and there is a sufficiently large group of people needing such training; or individualistic pairing procedures inside the school, which would be relevant where staff are requesting very specific skill training where those skills are already possessed by other members of the school staff and where those skills can be demonstrated in the ordinary course of events. So for example Foster and Thompson (1991) describe situations in which when two members of staff were involved in a joint discussion with parents and children about a specific bullying incident, the two members of staff consist of one more experienced member and one more junior member.

A further source of training which should not be ignored is the 'old fashioned' practice of encouraging individual members of staff to undertake significant individual projects on behalf of the school as a part of an externally provided course, for example a higher degree course. The reason why such individual projects have tended to be seen as unproductive in the past is that they were often unrelated to any of the general interests of the school. This was often very much regretted by the people undertaking such projects. When the project however is designed to be an integral part of work which has to be done to develop the policy, or to evaluate its effectiveness, then the energy and commitment provided by such individually based work can be extremely useful. A further advantage of this is of course that the person completing the project is likely to have specialised support from external consultants in the higher educational institution.

## Using external consultants

Schools can use consultants either as 'technical consultants' where the consultant is providing specific advice, methods and models to explain to school staff how to do something; or they can be used as, 'process consultants' where their main function is to take part in school communication processes in order to improve the effectiveness of the communication and to encourage staff to work together on common concerns by providing a cross-departmental framework. When they are used in the former capacity their input can be restricted to one or two specific sessions, often of a fairly standard in-service training format, where the consultants talk about the background theory of the methods concerned, give some practical examples of how the methods have been applied elsewhere, and then finish the training session by taking the staff present through a discussion session involving specific data from the school concerned to illustrate how the methods may be applied in this specific context. This 'technical' use of consultants could be appropriate in the areas of assessing how common bullying was in the school, demonstrating particular intervention strategies at various points in the bullying process, or running a workshop on how to identify bullying behaviour from more general aggression. If the project management team feels themselves reluctant to involve any particular group in school – for example, the parents – in the consultations of the anti-bullying policy, then the outside consultants may be extremely useful as 'process' consultants. Typically they would first discuss with individual staff members the current practices in school for involving parents, in order to clarify in their own mind what was happening at present; and then they would go on to either set up meetings jointly with members of staff, or participate in a series of meetings between parents and staff which the staff had set up. They may have a formal role in such meetings, such as chair or minutes secretary; or they may be present solely as an external person who has the freedom to ask questions and invite discussion on topics which the others present may feel uncomfortable with and may therefore skate over without addressing issues actually present. As such a series of meetings developed, and the joint agenda was more completely understood by those participating in the meeting, then the consultant would tend to fade into the background and leave the communication channels more or less open. Further examples of process consultation might be to involve them in training of lunchtime supervisors alongside a couple of members of the school teaching staff who will be forming part of the support for the lunchtime supervisors in implementing the anti-bullying policy on the playground; or involving them in the processes of consulting the children on the content of the anti-bullying policy.

Whenever involving consultants, it is usually useful for a number of members of staff in the school, specifically the project management group, to have a fairly clear idea as to why they are involving consultants in the first place. A good consultant will immediately try to clarify precisely what is needed in the opening meeting, if the school have not indicated their needs adequately beforehand. However, not all consultants may be as meticulous as this, and in any case it speeds up the process for the school to have thought through what they want from the consultant beforehand. This at least provides a good basis for discussion. The possible consultants for most schools would come from three sources, local education authority support teams such as behaviour support teachers, advisers, and educational psychologists; staff of local higher and further education institutions who have some contact with the school or with the particular issue concerned; and the various private agencies which are beginning to establish themselves to deliver in-service training on a commercial basis. They should all operate reasonably similarly, although the brochures of the private agencies will probably be glossier and have more colour pictures in them than those of the two other groups. On the other hand, members of the two other groups may make little or no financial demand on the school, seeing the consultation work as an extension of their existing contacts with the school. Whatever the institutional base of the consultants, their role should be clearly one of helping school staffs to understand the processes involved in setting up whole school policies and ensuring that the school staffs can carry out the procedures.

## Evaluation of the in-service training

The key question when considering how to evaluate in-service training is definitely not 'how shall we do it?' but 'what are we evaluating in-service training for?' If the purpose of the evaluation is not clear from the beginning in quite specific terms and often posing quite specific questions, it is quite unlikely that the evaluation will be of any use at all. The first question in any evaluation is always 'what do those running the evaluation wish to know about the in-service training?' The methods then follow on from the answers to that question. The purposes of the evaluation are usually to give a critical comment on the conduct and methods of delivery of the training events themselves (course evaluation); to find out if the par-ticants have learned something new which is now informing their practice (output evaluation); and to assess how far the in-service training was related to actual changes in school life. This is usually called impact evaluation and is the most difficult of the three to achieve effectively. It certainly needs a much longer time period over which to assess change. When considering impact evaluation of staff training designed to support a whole school policy, the impact of the training may also become confused with the impact of the policy itself. So, for example, it is quite possible that some in-service training associated with an anti-bullying policy might involve workshops for staff on methods of responding to complaints of victimisation received from pupils. If this is effective, it is quite reasonable to expect that over a period of time (6 to 12 months) children's attitudes to telling teachers when victimisation is occurring in school may change, and a much higher proportion of children may be prepared to tell the teaching staff. However, other elements of the whole school policy such as particular anti-bullying class or school rules may be also emphasising the same activities, that when children are involved as victims or when they see other people being victimised they should inform the teaching staff. In practice, it is probably better to assume that the impact evaluation of staff education and training is better dealt with as one contribution to the evaluation of effectiveness of the overall policy. Training evaluation then would probably be limited to course evaluation and output evaluation. Evaluation can be somewhat of a technical subject if the most useful information is desired, and so it may be one that the consultants can help with quite appreciably. The key question remains however 'who needs the information, how will the information help the refinement of the staff development process, and how can confidentiality be protected?'.

CHAPTER 7

# Whole School Policies in Operation – Lessons Learned from the Sheffield Anti-Bullying Project

In this chapter we will examine the process described so far using examples from primary and secondary schools who have been directly involved in or associated with the DfE funded Sheffield Anti-Bullying Project. Each of the sixteen primary and seven secondary schools who were involved in the project established a whole school anti-bullying policy as a core intervention. These policies proved to be the central feature of effective action against bullying and it was clear from the evaluation of these that it was not only the content of the policy which mattered but also the way in which it was developed (Sharp and Thompson, 1994). Similar conclusions have been drawn from other anti-bullying initiatives (Roland, 1993, Smith, 1994).

## The Sheffield anti-bullying project

The DfE funded Sheffield Anti-Bullying Project represented the first major study in the U.K. concerned with bullying. On an international basis it has made a significant contribution to research, establishing not only a baseline of data on levels of bullying but also by confirming that intervention against bullying can be effective.

The Sheffield Project was directed by Professor Peter Smith in the Department of Psychology at Sheffield University. A project team, representing a cross section of specialists in different areas, provided a 'think tank' to help shape and refine the project design and analysis. The project itself built upon data from an initial survey into the nature and extent of bullying in Sheffield schools which had been funded by the Calouste

Gulbenkian Foundation (Whitney and Smith, 1993). This first survey used an adapted version of the questionnaire developed for Dan Olweus's pioneering study in Norway (Olweus, 1991). The study also used Olweus's definition of bullying in introducing the idea of bullying behaviour to students before they completed the questionnaire: 'A student is being bullied or picked on when another student or group of students says nasty things to him or her. It is also bullying when a student is hit, kicked, threatened, locked inside a room, sent nasty notes, when no-one ever talks to them and things like that.' Forms of aggression which involve two people or groups of people of equal strength or power who are having an occasional disagreement or fight were not classed as bullying behaviour.

## The Results of the First Survey

Twenty-four schools took part in the initial survey, involving a total of 2,623 primary aged students and 4,135 secondary aged students. The schools were selected to represent a cross section of the general population in terms of socio-economic and environmental factors.

The data emerging from the survey demonstrated that bullying was widespread in both secondary and primary schools. On average, 10 per cent of secondary school and 27 per cent of primary school students reported that they had been bullied more than once or twice during the school term leading up to the survey. Alarmingly, 4 per cent of secondary aged students and 10 per cent of primary aged students reported being bullied consistently throughout the term. This small group of very badly bullied students were also more likely to be bullied on their journey to and from school. Most bullying took place around the school, especially in the playground areas. The most common forms of bullying involved name calling, physical aggression, social exclusion and spreading nasty rumours.

In addition to describing the nature and extent of bullying behaviour, the study highlighted how reluctant students were to tell a member of teaching staff when they were being bullied. This 'secrecy' made it difficult for teachers to detect bullying behaviour and, indeed, when presented with the survey results for their schools most staff were shocked and surprised to discover how much bullying was going on. This first survey indicated that parents were usually the first adults to learn of bullying behaviour.

## The Structure of the Project

Having been presented with a 'bullying profile' for their individual school, twenty-three of the original twenty-four agreed to continue with a more extensive intervention project. This project aimed to identify, through evaluation, what kinds of measures were effective against bullying. As already mentioned, all of the schools undertook to establish a whole school anti-bullying policy. They also appointed a project co-ordinator from their staff who would act as a direct link with the project team and who would oversee developments within the school. In both primary and secondary schools, this person was often a senior manager. Although the anti-bullying initiative was identified as a priority within each school, in no case was the project co-ordinator allocated extra time to manage the project, nor were financial resources provided by the project to enable this to happen. The project aimed to identify what schools could realistically achieve. The only financing of staff time provided by the project was directed at funding training for lunchtime supervisors.

Schools could also choose to implement a range of more localised interventions. These interventions were chosen to represent the kinds of approaches and materials readily available to schools at the outset of the project. Only those interventions which were accessible and achievable by any normal school were considered. The project was intended to be replicable and therefore any intervention which involved too much resourcing or unrealistic levels of support to introduce and maintain were not included. The additional interventions fell into three broad categories. These were:

● Curriculum based interventions, using materials or approaches which promoted or directly taught anti-bullying values.
● Methods for direct intervention in bullying situations.
● Strategies for enhancing the quality of playtimes and lunchbreaks.

The schools were supported in implementing both the whole school policy development and the optional interventions in a number of ways. Firstly, they were given access to training from recognised experts in each of the interventions. Although the cost of the training itself was borne by the project, schools had to provide their own cover to enable staff to attend. They were also provided with copies of recommended materials. These included a copy of the booklet 'Bullying: a positive response' by Tattum and Herbert, a copy of the A.C.E. advice sheet for governors on tackling bullying and a copy of the book edited by Peter Smith and David Thompson, 'Practical Approaches to Bullying'. Both the booklet and broadsheet have been distributed to schools throughout England, Wales and Northern Ireland in a joint initiative by the Calouste Gulbenkian Foundation and British Telecom. Other materials related to specific interventions such as the video produced by Central T.V. *Sticks and Stones*, the video of the Neti-Neti Theatre Company's play, *Only Playing Miss!*, and a copy of the story book by Arvan Kumar, *'The Heartstone Odyssey'*.

In addition to the initial training and materials, project co-ordinators were encouraged to attend termly support meetings which provided a forum for discussion about core themes and allowed the sharing of ideas and solutions. These more often than not related to the development and implementation of the whole school anti-bullying policy. Again, schools financed the release of co-ordinators themselves.

Each school was visited half termly by the research associate who was in fact an educational psychologist. This visit, which usually lasted less than one hour, had a dual purpose of monitoring the school's progress and supporting the school in planning and clarifying future direction. During these visits, the project co-ordinator was able to reflect upon recent developments, discuss problem areas and set short and long term goals. The research associate often shared relevant information. This related either to other schools in the project who were at a similar stage of intervention or who had faced similar difficulties, or national and even international developments which the school might wish to replicate. Sometimes the research associate would be able to put one school in contact with another school and a certain degree of informal networking did occur between schools.

As schools progressed through the policy development process, it was common for individual or groups of staff to identify personal training needs. Again, the research associate would assist the school in meeting these needs either by directing the staff towards existing training materials or courses or by running 'in house' training events.

*Monitoring*

The project team regularly and systematically collected data about what the schools had actually done and how much time this had taken. In relation to whole school policy development and implementation, two thirds of staff in each primary school and one third of secondary staff were interviewed towards the end of the project. These interviews investigated the extent to which each member of staff had been actively involved in the different phases of policy development and implementation; their perceptions of most and least successful practice in relation to this; and their views on changes in the school culture and the behaviour of themselves, their colleagues and students, as a result of intervention through the establishment of an anti-bullying policy.

All students over the age of seven completed the survey questionnaire in November 1993 (two years after the original survey). In selected schools, some students were interviewed and all parents were invited to complete a questionnaire about their involvement in policy development. Levels of bullying over time were monitored by termly sampling of key year groups. Each additional intervention had its own specifically designed monitoring procedure which typically involved some of the students who had directly experienced an intervention completing questionnaires or being interviewed.

*The Outcomes of the Project*

Analysis of the data emerging from the project established that the more effort schools put into tackling the problem of bullying, the more likely they are to reduce the amount of bullying which occurs. The establishment of a whole school policy against bullying behaviour emerged as a core feature of intervention.

Schools within the project experienced an increase in the number of students who would tell a teacher when they were being bullied; a decrease in the number of students who report actually being bullied or bullying others; and an increase in the number of students who said they would help if they knew that a peer was being bullied. In very active schools, the majority of students were aware that the school were trying to prevent and reduce bullying behaviour. They also felt that the school had been successful in achieving this.

The degree of reduction in levels of bullying differed between primary and secondary schools. Primary schools saw bigger reductions in levels of reported bullying behaviour sooner. In secondary schools, progress was slower and less visible although other changes, such as increased numbers of students telling a teacher when they had been bullied, were immediately noticeable Part of this differing rate of change is attributable to size but some of it may be related to the existence of alternative cultures between the two phases brought about by organisational features. In the secondary sector, divisions between groups of staff are more prevalent – therefore making involvement and discussion more cumbersome. There is little continuous or lengthy contact with individual students and the emphasis in much of the curriculum is subject oriented rather than concerned with social development. The primary sector has an advantage in its ability to facilitate face to face discussion involving all staff. Individual teachers are able to build up an intensive relationship with each student over a year. This offers much greater group stability and allows the teacher more influence over class culture and group values. Social themes can be pursued at length and integrated in a cohesive manner throughout the curriculum. Evidence from longer studies of school influence on bullying behaviour (Thompson and Arora, 1991, Roland, 1993) indicates that secondary schools can achieve such change but that it takes longer and more consistent effort to realise.

The most successful schools were those which:

- Made tackling bullying a high priority issue with visible commitment from the head teacher, governors and senior managers.
- Appointed a high status and proven facilitator as project co-ordinator such as the head teacher, deputy head, or a member of the senior management team.

- Involved *all* staff actively in the development of a whole school anti-bullying policy through awareness raising and discussion based consultation procedures.
- Included students and their families in opportunities for discussion about the problem of bullying and the way in which the school should tackle it, as well as deliberately fostering a sense of collective responsibility for tackling bullying behaviour.
- Made training in direct interventions accessible to all staff (including lunchtime supervisors) and encouraged attendance at such training events.
- Ensured the continued implementation of the policy through providing a long term programme of staff training and discussion; deliberate and planned promotion of anti-bullying values and teaching of anti-bullying strategies through curriculum content and delivery; regular monitoring of levels of bullying and periodic review of existing procedures.

**The process of policy development**

The most effective schools abandoned the more typical approach to policy development which involved the delegation of policy creation to a sub-group of interested or relevant people who would disappear for a number of meetings and reappear with a ready made policy document. 'Consultation' had previously often been no more than an opportunity for other staff to read the document and comment in writing. The policy would then be assigned to the staff handbook. Instead, the successful schools progressed through a very clear, iterative process of planning and preparation; awareness raising; consultation; policy drafting and redrafting; implementation and review. At the outset of the project all of the schools had recognised the importance of certain features of this process – the consultation with people other than teaching staff; the need to communicate and review. However, the clearly defined stages of the process had not been articulated or described, nor had the importance of this process been fully recognised. In retrospect, it is clear not only from the Sheffield Project but also from other similar projects (Olweus, 1993, Pepler *et al,* 1993, Roland, 1993, Smith,. 1994), that schools who do not follow this kind of intensive and thorough process are unlikely to make much impact upon student or staff behaviour either immediately or in the long term. Whilst school staffs may say 'We cannot afford to spend so much time and effort on a behaviour/special needs policy', we strongly advise that schools cannot afford not to and even suggest that it is a waste of time to do anything else.

**Planning and preparation**

Schools are busy places and teachers are busy people. All kinds of issues and initiatives constantly vie for attention and priority. To keep a behaviour or equal opportunities policy high profile it is better to have planned ahead and booked essential development time throughout the school calendar. The whole process of establishing an effective policy is likely to take a year and the policy will need to be the main topic on several staff and governor meeting agendas. Maintenance and review will require time every year thereafter. These kinds of policies have to be integrated into the ongoing school development plan so they do not become lost or forgotten, and to assist the school in adopting a constant 'inoculation against bullying' approach.

Initially the head teachers and senior managers will have to identify who will co-ordinate the policy development process. In the Sheffield project we found that the most successful co-ordinators were senior managers who were enthusiastic about tackling the problem, supported by a small working group drawn from teaching and non-teaching staff, governors and parents. Existing support agents, such as Educational Psychologists, Behaviour Support Team members and local Police Officers were also involved. The brief of this group was clearly defined from the outset. Reporting structures to the rest of the school community were also established. This nucleus group of people were to become the energisers and motivators of the wider community. It was important that they quickly became well informed about the nature of the problem to be tackled and familiarised themselves with appropriate literature, materials and examples of good practice in other schools. They therefore become a school based group of 'experts'.

From their informed position, this working group can begin to chart how the school will progress over the next twelve to eighteen months. They have to identify how and when each stage of the establishment process will occur. In planning, they must strive to achieve a good balance between opportunities for discussion and deliberation and maintaining momentum. Effective schools in Sheffield harnessed the energy and confidence about the issue generated by an INSET day by beginning the consultation process immediately afterwards. The latter part of the INSET was spent designing how staff, students and parents should be consulted with. They maintained the energy by quickly transforming people's comments into a first draft document, within which individuals were easily able to recognise their own contributions. To be able to spend sufficient time on consultation as well as move quickly through the development process needs forethought, planning and good organisation.

**Awareness raising**

Informing people about the nature of the problem and how it can and should be tackled is an essential precursor to consultation. Awareness raising activities should be offered to all sections of the community, beginning with staff. A popular model for awareness raising in the Sheffield schools was for all staff to attend a school based training session on bullying. Each member of staff would then engage in a similar process with tutor groups or classes and parents meetings. This works well as long as staff feel sufficiently informed about the problem themselves and have clearly identified the aims of working with students and parents in this way.

Awareness raising meetings and training events took many different forms. The best and most helpful were based upon a whole day of INSET training and involved all staff (including non-teaching staff) and governors. They were run by someone who was accepted by the participants as an 'expert'. This 'expert' role was sometimes held by someone within the school community or by an invited outsider. By the end of the day each participant felt that they understood what bullying is, why it was important to tackle the problem and what could be done about it on an individual and whole school basis. They were also clear about what the school was trying to achieve over the next twelve months, how this was going to be achieved and their role within that process. The day gave them a good knowledge base and a sense of direction.

Most of these training events were underpinned by an explicit set of values and offered a standard set of information. The values and attitudes being promoted through the day were that:

● bullying behaviour in any form is unacceptable (including staff bullying);
● it is important to tackle minor forms of bullying before they escalate into more extreme aggressive behaviour;
● 'good' schools do something about bullying.

The range of information offered invariably included general data from studies about bullying (Whitney and Smith, 1993, Besag, 1989) – what kinds of behaviours constitute bullying; how often it occurs; where it occurs; contributing factors. It emerged that it was particularly helpful to include factual information about levels of bullying within that school, ascertained via student surveys. This kind of survey obviously has to be administered and analysed prior to the training day. Having a factual data base which relates directly to the school is a highly motivating force for action. Many staff will be surprised to find out exactly how much bullying is happening.

We found that most staff, however cynical about the likelihood of change, accepted that bullying was not a good thing for children to experience. This was certainly the view of most students and most parents.

However, from here onwards there was usually a range of views and attitudes about the nature of bullying and how it should be prevented and responded to. Bullying takes many different forms and most people will have quite clear opinions about what is serious bullying and what is not. Some staff may dismiss the more subtle psychological and indirect forms of bullying, arguing that if they were expected to respond to every minor incident they would never be able to get on with teaching. For these staff, it is worthwhile pointing out that an early response to 'low level' bullying not only communicates to students that the school takes all forms of bullying seriously but also stops the escalation of bullying behaviour to more aggressive forms. If we unravel some of the more extreme acts of violence which have occurred in U.K. schools recently, we will often find that the tension between students began with name calling, rumour mongering or social exclusion campaigns. Similarly there may be differences of opinion regarding how bullying should be prevented or responded to. We would recommend that the school develops a graded response system of rewards for co-operative behaviour and sanctions for hostile behaviour. The bottom line must be that every member of staff must make some immediate response to any act of aggression, intimidation or harassment no matter how minor. This does not mean that there has to be a high level of response but that they simply make it clear that the behaviour has been noted and that it is not acceptable. Building on from this initial response, there needs to be a clear set of procedures for responding to persistent bullying or more extreme violence, perhaps even involving the police when there is an assault or threat of assault (see Pitts (1993) for an example of this). The early involvement of parents is highly recommended.

## Consultation and policy drafting

Consultation with staff and governors necessitated the use of meetings and staff development time. Some schools did resort to circulating a draft document for comment but the most effective schools allowed time for discussion and debate, either as a whole staff or in small groups, as well as opportunities for staff to individually write down what they felt the school's response to bullying should be. It is worthwhile noting that they were actually given a specific time to do this, e.g. 'In the next hour, instead of a normal staff meeting, each of you should go somewhere quiet and think about what you personally feel we should be doing to tackle the problem of bullying. Write down your thoughts and give them to X.' By providing this time for individual reflection and brainstorming, all staff and governors were able to contribute their ideas rather than simply the most vocal. In our analysis of the data arising from the Sheffield project, thorough involvement of all staff in the consultation and awareness raising process correlated highly significantly with a reduction in levels of bullying.

*Involving Students*

Involvement of students in the consultation process required a little more organisation but, given that they are a captive audience, was not too difficult to achieve. Most schools manipulated some part of the timetable to facilitate consultation. It was common for consultation to follow directly on from awareness raising work which would involve students in discussion of what bullying is, their experiences of bullying, the moral dilemmas faced by students who witness or are indirectly involved in' bullying I and so on. The students were then asked exactly the same question as the teaching and non-teaching staff: 'What do you think our school should do to prevent and respond to bullying?' Schools varied whether they involved students from the outset or presented them with a draft to work from. Their ideas were collated by the co-ordinator.

There were some immediately visible effects of this awareness raising and consultation process with students. All schools reported an increase in students telling a member of staff if they or a peer was being bullied. This helped the staff be more responsive to bullying situations and intervene at an earlier stage. Staff reported that students generally began to be more concerned about the welfare of their peers -- they were more likely to intervene if they knew another student was unhappy. The students began to share responsibility for taking action against bullying behaviour with staff. Bullying was no longer seen as something that 'the teachers should sort out'. This change in attitude was probably due to the increasing emphasis placed on 'bystanders' by the schools in the project as well as a response to the very act of consultation.

It was clear from the data from the initial survey that many students were aware that bullying was happening and who was doing what to whom. It was also evident that there were specific classes within each school which had relatively high levels of bullying compared to other classes within the same year group. If we examine the dynamics of some of these high level bullying classes we may find that there is often a very cohesive and mutually supportive group of 'powerful' students who tend to bully each other and other students as part of their normal way of interacting. Also within the class there may be a small number of students who are regularly targeted by the powerful, bullying group. The other students may be less frequently picked on by the powerful group and may be wary of them. However, these bystanders may distance themselves from the victims, possibly even supporting the bullying behaviour at times by laughing at nasty names or by covering up for the more powerful gang if the teacher asks questions about what is going on. In contrast to the tight knit bullying group, the rest of the class is socially fragmented and unsupportive of each other. In the absence of encouragement to do otherwise, they too easily turn a blind eye to what is happening and in doing so collude with the bullying behaviour. Some project schools addressed this issue of bystanders by directly teaching students assertive strategies to use in a situation where a fellow student is being bullied. The notion that it is everybody's responsibility to take action against bullying was widely and regularly reinforced.

In one school in London with whom we have had close contact, the policy was entirely constructed by the students. They rejected more punitive responses-to bullying behaviour outright. They were also clear that exclusion was an unhelpful solution, pointing out that it was more of a *'cop out'* by the school and simply transferred the problem elsewhere. The pupil's response system was based on a counselling approach and included a 'buddy' system where a student who was persistently involved with bullying was linked to a responsible peer to help them change their behaviour.

## Involving Parents

Involving parents was more difficult to achieve and schools had to invest considerable effort in doing this. Parents whose children had been bullied were understandably very keen to take an active role in helping the school take action against bullying. However, this was at most 20 per cent of parents. Most schools had to adopt creative and diverse approaches to engaging parents in discussion and be pro-active in making contact with them. Opportunities for discussion were generally more effective than written contact. Most schools had to use more than one method to reach the majority of parents. These included parent questionnaires, parent workshops, open assemblies, newsletters, plays about bullying, home visits. One secondary school used the students as intermediaries. As part of the awareness raising and consultation work with students, each child was provided with a set of questions relating to the policy for discussion with their parents. This was set as homework for every child in the school. The next lesson they fed back what the views of their parents had been. Another school was determined to contact every parent and so held a number of different kinds of meetings in school and kept a note of who had attended. Parents who had not been present were contacted by letter.

## Redrafting

The intensity of the consultation process is greater at the outset. People's initial comments are often more detailed and lengthy. Most schools produced several drafts – each draft being scrutinised by all staff, students and some parents. Students in particular were helpful in ensuring that the strategies suggested were likely to be effective and keeping the document clear and easily understood.

**Implementation**

Implementing the policy involves communicating the policy widely – everyone must know what the policy means in practice. It is worthwhile spelling this out clearly to staff, governors, students and parents and reminding them at least once a term. We found that despite staff fears that the school would be *'overdoing'* it, a high profile policy emphasised to students that bullying behaviour was taken seriously by the school. This kind of reminder – whether delivered through classroom work or assembly – has a relatively short term effect. For a couple of weeks afterwards it encourages the majority of students to be more considerate towards each other and therefore cuts down on one off incidents of bullying behaviour. It makes many students more likely to tell someone if they or someone else is being bullied – it reminds them that teachers and other staff do want to know about bullying and that they themselves should help people who are being bullied. We have also found that this preventative kind of approach helps bullied students feel more supported and less vulnerable (Shah, 1993). However, it is naive to believe that this preventative approach will stop persistent bullying. More direct and long term action is required to achieve that kind of change. Successful interventions with students who more persistently bully others include the design and implementation of a behaviour modification programme, counselling and involvement of parents.

Often, to be able to implement the policy, there is a need for training or development of materials. For example, most schools agreed that one effective way of preventing bullying was to use the curriculum to promote anti-bullying values and to teach anti-bullying behaviour. This requires each subject or class teacher to scrutinise the curriculum and identify where and how this will be achieved. We found that in terms of addressing bullying through the curriculum, most teachers felt confident and able to do this. They could identify specific resources which related to bullying an incident in history or current affairs, a choice of story or poem, or alternatively would use curriculum methods which emphasised the need to work co-operatively together and allowed time for personal reflection on and evaluation of individual and group behaviour. They felt less confident, however, when it came to responding directly to a bullying incident, either in terms of supporting the bullied student, dealing with the perpetrators of the bullying, or tackling the issue on a whole class basis when there was a bullying ethos within a group. There was a clear need for most, if not all, staff to be involved in training to specifically deal with these kinds of situations. When provided, there was a general consensus of how useful and empowering such training was. Even some staff who tended to be more directly aggressive with students (and colleagues) conceded that previously their aggressiveness had been partially related to them not knowing what else to do. The training in assertion and negotiation skills had extended their repertoire of possible reactions and that consequently they had modified their behaviour.

*Response to Incidents of Bullying*

Implementing the policy means not only preventing bullying via the promotion of anti-bullying values in the curriculum, but also responding efficiently to bullying incidents when they arise. All staff must be seen to listen and investigate alleged bullying, whether it is reported by parents, the bullied person or a concerned bystander. We have found that problem solving approaches which do not apportion blame are most effective. In the Sheffield project we used 'The Method of Shared Concern', developed by Swedish psychologist Anatol Pikas (Pikas, 1989). A similar method has recently been developed in the U.K. called 'The No-Blame Approach' (Maines and Robinson, 1993). These kinds of approaches, which are based on conflict resolution, allow the teacher or supervisor to take the problem seriously and help the students involved to find a solution without pushing either party into a defensive or unco-operative position. The adult acknowledges from the outset that there is a problem and asks each individual to suggest a way of changing the situation. This kind of approach places the responsibility for change with the students. It neither punishes nor renders the bullied student 'helpless'. It also saves the adult from becoming entangled in a hopeless investigation whereby each child sticks adamantly to their version of the 'truth' and are both equally convincing. Open communication with all sets of parents from the outset smoothes home-school relationships and reinforces the image of a caring school. Parental' involvement also makes student behaviour change more likely to occur.

Prompt and efficient action makes students feel more confident in the school and enhances the safeness of the school environment. The knowledge that action will be taken not only emboldens more students to tell if they are being bullied but also acts as a deterrent for students considering bullying others. In a small school or primary school, where student teacher relationships are highly visible, the effect of an implemented policy on levels of bullying is fairly rapid. In larger schools, where school response to bullying behaviour will only be noted by a small percentage of the whole population the duration of bullying incidents should drop. Instead of bullying going on for weeks, the students should be reporting the problem to teachers at an early stage.

*Monitoring the Effect of the Policy*

Schools can only find out how effectively their policies are being implemented by introducing some kind of monitoring procedures. In the

Sheffield project schools, a repeat survey allowed assessment of change. Many schools we have worked with have introduced an annual screening procedure which provides valuable information about patterns of bullying behaviour and allows success in tackling the problem to be evaluated.

Staff, students and parents can be asked to identify ways of refining existing systems. This continuous evaluation of progress is important in reminding staff, parents and students of the school's anti-bullying approach and in maintaining motivation to take action. It also helps schools to answer the question posed in inspections: *'How do you know your policy works?'*.

Screening processes usually involve the administration of some kind of questionnaire-based survey. These will usually set out to identify how much and what kind of bullying is happening, how long it has gone on for, who (in terms of gender/race/age) has been involved, where it has happened. Schools can develop their own questionnaires, and students themselves can usefully be involved in this, although there are benefits in using an established screening tool such as the 'Life in Schools Checklist' (Arora, 1994) or the questionnaire devised by Olweus and used in the Sheffield Project (Whitney and Smith, 1993). These questionnaires have been tried and tested and are known to be reliable. They also allow schools to compare themselves with data collected from other schools. After one year of intervention, schools can expect to find a reduction in the duration of bullying behaviour, an increase in the number of children who will tell a teacher or another member of staff, an increase in the number of students who would do something to help a fellow student who was being bullied and that the majority (over 80 per cent) of students perceive that the school takes action against bullying. With continued effort, in subsequent years, schools should see a drop of up to 50 per cent in levels of bullying. Primary schools and smaller secondary schools are likely to see reductions in levels of bullying at an earlier stage. We are fortunate in having contact with a small number of schools who have been tackling bullying for a number of years. One secondary school, in Sweden, uses the Olweus questionnaire at the beginning and end of every year. They find that levels of bullying are high amongst their Year 7 students on entry and they have an intensive programme of curriculum work against bullying in the first term. By the end of the year levels of bullying reported in the survey have fallen by 50 per cent, although they have never been able to reduce the bullying beyond this level. This reduction is considerably higher than the expected reduction over a year of 15 per cent (Whitney and Smith, 1993). They have found that from Year 7 onwards, levels of bullying remain low but never completely disappear. If a new student enters at any point during the school year, there is usually an increase in levels of bullying behaviour in that group of students. Staff have begun to take preventative action when a new student arrives and monitor their progress carefully.

Some schools in the Sheffield project adopted some of the other monitoring procedures used by the project team. The most popular was a termly sampling procedure which involved students in particular classes completing a short questionnaire every day for a week on return into the class after lunch. The questionnaire gave a list of bullying behaviours and asked students to indicate whether or not they had experienced these behaviours that day. This procedure was repeated in the same week of each term with the same students. Drops of 40 per cent in bullying behaviour were identifiable. These reductions were well above the expected fall in levels of bullying behaviour of 15 per cent per year. Other schools involved all adults (especially lunchtime supervisors) in recording every incident of bullying behaviour, no matter how minor, reported to them during one week. This enabled a profile of bullying behaviour to be built up. A repeat of the same process at a later stage, but at the same time of the year or term, yields comparison data.

Additional information can also be gained from recording incidents of bullying which have been reported. Clearly there are ethical issues relating to data protection and cases where bullying has been alleged but not proven (often the majority of cases) to be considered by schools who are going to introduce such a system. However, a record of the age, gender and race of the students involved as well as the date and nature of action taken and follow up can be helpful in identifying students who are persistently involved in bullying behaviour (either on the receiving end or as perpetrators) or in gauging the success of focussed intervention with a group of students. This kind of information can also be compared with survey data to assess how successfully bullying is being picked up by the school staff.

One important feature of monitoring specific incidents of bullying is the follow up procedures. The school must be sure that once a bullying situation has been identified and action has been taken that the bullying does not re-occur. It is not sufficient for staff to rely upon the bullied student to re-report if the bullying starts again. Regular checks initiated by a member of staff, involving the students and parents, ensures a speedy response to a reoccurrence but more importantly communicates to all parties that the bullying is taken seriously.

## Review

Is a policy which relates to a social aspect of school life ever 'finished'? We doubt it. Annual review procedures provide a forum for reflection and change. Most schools in the Sheffield project have found that there was a need for refining of systems and for modification of practice. The review process should also serve to remind staff, governors and parents of the school's stance against bullying and provide an opportunity for new staff to become engaged in the important awareness raising and discussion processes which are linked to successful implementation.

As in the earlier stages of policy development, policy review is not confined to a small group of staff but should re-involve the whole school community. By issuing an invitation to parents and students as well as staff and governors to comment on the policy in practice, the school can identify ways in which the policy has been successful and areas in which it needs further development. The data collected from the annual screening provides a factual base for evaluation and discussion. Training needs for staff over the coming year can be identified; curriculum review can highlight the effectiveness of preventative work with students. One outcome of the review process should be the identification of short and long term goals for the future. These goals can then be integrated into the school development plan.

**Difficulties in developing a whole school anti-bullying policy**

The major factors which hinder policy development and implementation relate to the organisational and managerial features of the school and the priority which is placed upon developing such a policy by the head teacher and governors. Progress will also depend upon the skills of the policy coordinator in motivating staff, in preparing the school for the development process and in ensuring that transition through the process is efficient. Head teachers should not allocate the role of co-ordinator to a person who is not equipped to fulfil it.

Without visible commitment from the head teacher, governors and senior management to the establishment of a whole school anti-bullying policy there simply will not be the opportunities for staff involvement necessary to achieve it. 'Visible commitment' requires continuing encouragement, resourcing and monitoring of the process not only in the development stage but also once the policy is being implemented and reviewed. Where the head teacher or senior managers take a half-hearted or dismissive approach to the policy development, progress is fragmentary and superficial and the effects minimal.

The rate of policy development is important and will influence the reactions of staff, students and parents to the policy itself. If policy development is too quick, involvement of the whole school community is likely to be superficial and response to change unnecessarily negative. However, if the process is too slow, energy and enthusiasm can wane with dissatisfaction and frustration setting in instead. Pre-planning of each stage which ensures efficient collation of ideas arising from consultation combined with effective communication of developments in progress can reduce these tensions.

Difficulties nearly always arise when only a small number of staff are directly and actively involved in policy development. This leads to poor understanding and knowledge of the policy and inconsistency in its implementation. Opportunities for staff involvement in policy development and adequate preparation of staff to discuss the issue of bullying with students and parents are essential. Without dialogue about bullying between staff, students and their families the impact of the policy on school culture is reduced. Students will only tell staff about bullying if they know they will be listened to. Students will only be careful of their own behaviour if they are sure their efforts to do so will be valued and that their transgressions will be responded to. They will only be able to handle more difficult aspects of their relationships constructively if they are taught how to do so. Similarly, families who are not aware of or do not fully understand the school's policy on bullying will not be able to support it. They are more likely to be defensive if it is implemented and their child is involved. They are also less likely to approach the school if their child is being bullied. This can lead to long term difficulties and resentment. It also undermines the image of the school as a safe learning environment. Bullying behaviour is far less likely to occur in a school where the collective and unified message of staff, students and their parents is 'Bullying is not O.K' and where this is reflected in general behaviour and interactions with others.

Changes in school staffing or student population can delay or redirect policy development and implementation. This can be particularly problematic when there is a change of head teacher or where a single person charged with co-ordinating policy development leaves or can no longer maintain the momentum for personal reasons. Schools can reduce the effects of these kinds of changes by working hard to maintain the profile of the policy and by maximising staff and student involvement. Where bullying is everyone's concern then policy development and implementation will, to a certain extent, establish its own momentum. Regular communication about the policy, effective review procedures and induction for staff, students and parents which actively promotes the policy and spells out what it means for each individual are essential.

## Key features in successful intervention

In this final section, we will briefly recap on some important lessons learnt through the work of the DfE Sheffield Anti-Bullying Project.

### The Role of Senior Management

Senior managers, in particular the head teacher, must be seen to take a leading role in the school's anti-bullying approach. They should provide a clear sense of direction for the whole school community by establishing a common set of aims and by facilitating the meaningful involvement of staff, students, parents and governors. This will involve the allocation of time and resources to anti-bullying initiatives and policy development.

## The Adoption of a Participative, Whole Community Approach

The active involvement of all staff in policy development, implementation and review is essential. The involvement of students and parents is highly advisable. Bullying is a social phenomenon and as such can only be tackled by a participative approach which emphasises the collective responsibility of all, including bystanders, in preventing and responding to bullying.

## Skilling the Staff

All staff, including lunchtime supervisors and any other ancillary staff, must have access to training to help them feel confident in their ability to intervene in bullying situations. Assertive behaviour management skills and conflict resolution strategies underpin most successful interventions in bullying incidents.

## Intervention at Every Level Within the School

The policy must define how bullying will be tackled and identify ways in which this can be achieved throughout the school. This means that not only are all the people within the school involved in preventing and responding to bullying, but also that different contexts are targeted: the classroom, the corridors and toilets, the playground, assemblies, the staff room. Intervention must be regular and frequent.

## The Anti-bullying Policy and Equal Opportunities

An anti-bullying policy, if implemented effectively, will reduce levels of bullying. Unless specifically designed to do so it will not prevent racially motivated aggression, sexual harassment or prejudice against people with disabilities. These issues have to be addressed in their own right. Effective schools will carefully integrate their approach to these different aspects of aggressive behaviour in schools so that collectively they provide a common framework for promoting co-operative behaviour and mutually respectful relationships amongst individuals and groups.

## Acknowledgement of Bullying Beyond the School Gates

The kind of 'whole community' anti-bullying policy advocated in this chapter impacts beyond the boundaries of the school day and of traditional teacher/parent/student relationships. Effective schools do take seriously bullying which occurs outside the school gates but which involves their students and have included in their policy details of how this will be responded to.

## The benefits of establishing a whole school anti-bullying policy

Schools who invest time and effort in the process of policy development and implementation will reap benefits. We have seen clearly that schools can reduce levels of bullying significantly and make themselves into safer learning environments. The process of policy development outlined here also has other positive outcomes. Because of the participative approach taken by a school, better relationships between teaching staff, non-teaching staff, students and parents become apparent. Systems of communication are strengthened and staff and students feel more confident to discuss sensitive issues. The image of the school as a caring and effective school is promoted. In short, the school becomes a more effective and successful community with a common set of aims and shared values which reject bullying behaviour and encourage co-operative relationships.

# CHAPTER 8

# Communication at the Chalk Face – Implementation of Behaviour Policies at the Year Level

## The year group in the school

In many schools both pastoral care and the discipline system is organised at the year level. In secondary schools the year team is often larger and may have more functions than in primary schools, although even there the year leader often has responsibility for being the first senior colleague with whom teachers raise concerns about children. The year leader at primary level is much more likely to have some aspects of curriculum coordination as a part of their general brief, although again some of the larger primary schools have given some responsibility for aspects of the curriculum to named specialists. Thinking of the year group as a social group, the year would consist of the children (possibly 100 to 150), the form tutors and the year tutor (possibly five to eight people altogether) and would include some members of the teaching staff as 'partial' members. The form tutors themselves will of course be subject teachers, also sometimes specifically with this year group and sometimes not. Those teachers who are not form tutors in this year will have some links with the year organisation, but will also spend probably the majority of their time elsewhere in the school, and at best could be seen as partial members of the year group as a whole. The overall clarity of identity of the year group as far as staff are concerned depends largely on the amount of time that the year tutors and the other teaching staff spend on this particular group of children. Some schools have a de-facto specialisation amongst their teaching staff, whereby some groups of teachers spend the bulk of their time with particular year groups. This can be because school policy has attempted to reduce the number of teachers whom the younger children in a secondary school have to deal with, or perhaps because the sixth form are taught by the more longer established or more highly academically qualified teachers. Where such partial age specialisation does exist, then it is more likely that the year group can develop a specific identity as a social group.

In a primary school, the year group's boundaries are stronger, because the staff teaching the children are very clearly identified and spend almost all their time with those children. At the same time, the relative smallness of the school as a whole means that both children and staff have relatively easier access to other children and teachers who are not part of their own year. The strength of the year group as a social group under these conditions will largely depend on the precise policies followed in school, and in particular the way in which year groups are treated as social units or not in general curricular and extra curricular activities.

**The role of the year team in implementing behaviour policies**

*Direct Responsibilities of the Year Staff*

Most schools expect year staff, the year tutor and the form tutors together, to be directly responsible for some aspects of implementation of behaviour policies. These would generally include responsibility for implementing the pastoral curriculum, or personal and social education, in so far as that happened in the tutor periods, as well as those aspects of presenting core values in the year assemblies. A second major area of responsibility is for sanctions and general disciplinary matters, in so far as these are involved in implementation of behaviour policies. Clearly the year team are operating here in the framework of general discipline policy agreed by the school, but as they act as one of the main supports for the class teachers their interpretation of sanctions and disciplinary procedures is crucial. They are usually much less involved with any linkage between the behaviour policies and subject teaching materials, except when due to school policy they are also heavily involved with subject teaching in their own particular year.

The year team may also be involved in the general issue of attendance monitoring, although practices differ from school to school as to who is the key point of contact for the education welfare officer when children are noticed as being unreasonably absent.

*Pastoral-Academic Staff Separation*

Practices differ between the schools on how distinct is the general split between staff principally involved with pastoral work and those whose non-teaching responsibilities take them in other directions such as curriculum co-ordination. In almost all schools some staff have specific responsibilities in either pastoral or curricular areas, but it is of course perfectly possible (although in average size schools difficult) for the same person to have both pastoral responsibilities either at the form tutor or year tutor level and some curriculum or departmental responsibilities. Many educationists have viewed the process of separation of the staff with primarily pastoral responsibilities from those with primarily curricular responsibilities with some horror, and many of the staff with pastoral responsibilities have been amongst them. In an ideal world, most teachers would agree that they should be able to both teach subjects to children and to act as I supportive adults in loco parentis with respect to the same children (Duncan, 1988, Best, Jarvis and Ribbins, 1984, Bulman, 1984).

However, in the real world, as opposed to the ideal one, school staffs have different personalities with different priorities and different career directions. Teachers are also under considerable pressure for efficiency and achieving ends with a certain economy of effort, and this almost invariably leads to a certain amount of specialisation. This means that at any one time certain teachers do have specific responsibilities on top of their class teaching for pastoral roles, and others have extra responsibilities for more curriculum centred roles. Each needs to recognise the validity of the others' responsibilities, and also sometimes to recognise the extra influence given by having a named role in the school, as well as the extra skills which may be developed by repeatedly dealing with similar issues. Sometimes this mutual respect for specific roles in school may be emphasised by a senior management team who expect that all the staff with any responsibilities in school should have had experience of both types of role, or even that staff with a more senior role in one area should also have a more junior role in another. For example, it is not uncommon to find schools where the heads of academic subject departments are also expected to act as form tutors, both to ensure that the overall management processes of the school do not become split into teams with only pastoral or academic interests, and to demonstrate by example to the more junior members of staff with minimal extra responsibilities that the senior management team sees expertise in both areas as being necessary to be an effective member of staff.

## Some crucial aspects of the year team's responsibilities for the effective implementation of whole school behaviour policies

One major theme of the devising and implementing whole school behaviour policies is the effective consultation and communication with children. Many of the topics of consultation are themselves emotionally loaded, and in practice many of the opportunities for consultation and discussion on these topics will occur during tutor periods. Because of this, the year tutor team plays a key part in raising the awareness of the children around the themes of whole school behaviour policies, managing the consultation discussions, and after the policy has been drawn up informing them of its content and implications. As a part of this general pattern of managing the formal communication with the children, the informal contacts that the year tutor team have with the children during the everyday incidents of school life also provide opportunities for expressing the disapproval of bullying and the other aggressive activities and building up an atmosphere of trust between the tutor team and the children. All teachers are interested in building the confidence of children, both in academic areas and in social areas, and effective implementation of the whole school behaviour policies involves building up the confidence of both the victimised children and the bystanders to communicate with the staff about the incidents occurring. School staff who do not have pastoral responsibilities for a particular year group but who only come into contact through subject teaching should also be involved in developing the confidence of children so that they will communicate emotionally sensitive issues to staff, but some such teachers may find that the time pressures of subject teaching in practice minimise the opportunities children have for communicating with them on non-subject matters. However, even if this is true during formal teaching periods, if the children feel that the staff members concerned are approachable, sensitive, and can be trusted to do something about their problem, the members of staff may find themselves approached in the corridors or playground. One of the findings of the research work on anti-bullying policies is that children do respond reasonably quickly to policies which expect children to communicate with staff more about bullying occurring, but that they are quite careful in selecting those individual members of staff whom they feel will take them seriously and who can be trusted to intervene appropriately in whatever situation is being discussed.

The year tutor team is also an important group for specifying their own training needs. As described above, an effective staff development programme involves needs surveys to establish need, but the senior management team also has to be aware of the development of staff knowledge and skills in areas which specifically influence events in school. A year tutor team is a significant portion of school staff centrally involved in the policy formulation and implementation, and hence in a very good position to determine their training needs to support effective policy implementation. Training may involve half days or days attendance at workshops away from school, or if the staff development needs assessment process is sufficiently integrated, there would be enough staff involved in tutor roles to form a significant group for an in-school training day.

The informal communication skills which the tutor teams develop when dealing with children in their year group are also central in the effective implementation of sanctions. The year tutor may often be involved as a main disciplinary representative of the school management at year level, even though the formal responsibility may lie elsewhere with the head of academic departments or assistant heads. Decisions on whether sanctions should be implemented, what sanctions are most appropriate, and which members of staff should be involved are often decided in discussion between the year tutor and either a subject teacher or a form tutor or the child concerned. Their knowledge, easy communication with the children, and consistency of interpretation of the policies are extremely important in effective policy implementation.

## Parent liaison

One of the tasks which year tutors in particular often find central to their role is effective parent liaison when particular children are having difficulties in school. The form of the difficulty can vary immensely, and in an ideal world again there obviously should be effective liaison between all parents and the people teaching their children, whether they had particular problems or not. The parent involvement element of implementing whole school behaviour policies means that this aspect of a year tutor's work again becomes central to effective policy implementation. Parents will develop long term relationships with key members of the tutor teams, and these relationships are particularly important if parents come from one of the ethnic minority groups in the school. Parents, children, and the school all need to find a common consensus on the value of educational activities, and the year tutor or form tutor as the main representative of the school in touch with their child gives parents a key point of contact. Where parents are convinced that school staff have the long term welfare of their children at heart, they are much more likely to support school and support their child to learn whilst at school, than where they see school staff as basically local representatives of an alien culture. To achieve this level of contact, tutors may well need to be prepared to visit parents at home rather than always expecting that parents should come to school for discussions, and be prepared to explain the reasons for educational practices in fairly straightforward terms. Additionally, language may prove a barrier, and finding and using interpreters is not a simple process. One common experience of tutors visiting homes in this way is that the fathers may be the parent with the influence in the home and with the better level of English language. If this is so, father's work schedule may be a major factor in the timing of home visits.

In many schools such home visits tend to fall to the year tutor. It may be true that they have a greater experience of the pastoral issues and of the problems of communicating with parents on emotionally sensitive matters, but that is no reason why they should be the only tutor to visit homes.

Others need to learn some of these skills, and the year tutor may be car-

120

rying a much greater general pastoral load than the individual form tutors would, with only minimal time released from the timetable to perform these duties. This may be an issue to be specifically addressed whilst the policies are being drawn up, and one where the guidance of the senior management team may be needed.

**Training for Home Visiting**

Communicating effectively with parents on emotionally tense issues is a new activity for many teachers, and some management teams are reluctant to encourage their staff to visit as a matter of course. Parent liaison is a central issue for many schools though, and usually the same management teams who are reluctant to encourage staff to visit know which members of staff they would trust to communicate effectively with parents over difficult issues. These staff are usually part of the pastoral care teams, who have developed their effectiveness with parents by a combination of initial interest and sensitivity, and practice. With an informal awareness of the training needs of more staff to become more confident in dealing with parents' concerns, the year tutors can develop a system of teamwork over home visiting that supports and legitimises younger teachers in their parental contacts.

To learn quickly and effectively, younger teachers need to be able to:

1. Discuss the purpose and possible outcomes of the visit.
2. Accept a change to the planned agenda when further issues are raised by parents.
3. Discuss matters with parents in an informal way, which allows parents to develop their own concerns and attitudes in a way which is difficult to do in school. Parents may well have past experiences of schools and teachers which make confident discussion for them on school grounds very difficult.
4. Recognise when parents are signalling that they wish to develop certain issues, but are reluctant to do it themselves – possibly because of lack of confidence in talking about these issues, or uncertainty as to whether the teacher would accept the concern as being a valid topic for discussion.
5. Recognise where the difference between the role of a teacher and a social worker lies. On first contact with the problems that some families are trying to cope with, some teachers may be tempted to see themselves as the sole helping agency. This is never the case, although some parental stresses can be directly helped by support in dealing with their children. School and its staff are representatives from the educational world, and their concerns are to do with effective education of the children concerned.

6. Recognise the legitimacy of, and reasons for, the differences in childrens' behaviour which occur between school and home. These behavioural differences may be very important in understanding the emotional world of the child, and hence in communicating with the child effectively in school.
7. Recognise that when a child realises that a member of the pastoral care staff has good contact with parents, and both share aims for the child's educational progress, that member of staff will develop greater influence J with that child in school.

All these skills are learned much more easily by visiting parents with a more experienced member of staff and discussing what happened in a fairly detailed way than by attending a short course on good pastoral care.

Systematic methods of family contact may help appreciably in establishing good parental liaison with particular sub-groups of children. These may be either all parents from ethnic minority groups, or all parents, or all parents whose children have given concern to staff elsewhere in the school. At this level, the contact may not need to be a formal visit – many parents are on the phone, and half an hour on the phone after six o'clock one evening may achieve initial contact with four or five families. If undertaken at the beginning of a new school year, or the beginning of the operation of a new tutor team, such informal contacts may make subsequent contacts a lot easier. The tutor calls simply to introduce themselves to the head of the family, and to extend the hand of welcome should the parents ever want to contact school about any educational matter. Parents, particularly from ethnic minority homes, may well have confused and inaccurate ideas of what to expect from fairly common events in school (such as a school visit to a local seaside town, or children entering for the Duke of Edinburgh's Award Scheme), and prior contact makes it easier for them to enquire.

Such parental contacts again are much easier if the school has developed a sensitive, public and accessible policy on such matters as school uniform, dress for physical education and swimming lessons, religious instruction, and any other matters which parents from a different cultural background may be concerned about. Duncan (1988) gives a good example of a uniform and physical education dress code which was evolved by Bradford L.E.A., which makes clear what modifications to the school uniform and physical education dress are acceptable where parents have cultural objections to girls in particular having limbs uncovered in public places.

The year tutor team may also wish to intervene by giving special attention to certain groups of children in their own informal contacts with the year group. These may be groups of especially vulnerable children, or groups who have particular needs for development of certain aspects of their social understandings and behaviour.

## How far can a year group be independent?

In some schools, an efficiently functioning year tutor team may wish to develop activities which are different from those pertaining in other years. Provided the procedures do not produce instances of minor chaos, and can be explained in an educationally appropriate way, there seems little reason why year teams should not develop different activities inside the areas indicated above, broadly the pastoral curriculum, supervision and sanctions, parent liaison. It helps of course if the form of organisation of the pastoral system is that type where the group of children has the same year tutor and form tutors as they move through the school. This avoids the children having to adjust to different patterns of pastoral activity at the end of the year. Clearly the senior management team would probably prefer that all year tutor teams operated to relatively similar practices, but this would require the development of effective whole school policies as described above, and if there is little enthusiasm in the school for development of such policies apart from one particular year group then it would seem unnecessarily damaging to staff morale in that year group to restrict their freedom of action. If developments do occur in one year group only then it would clearly be very helpful if the senior management team recognised the aims of the developments and used their best endeavours to ensure that the efforts of the particular year team were not actively interfered with by any members of staff seeing such developments as something of a threat to the status quo. It would be perfectly feasible to describe the operation as a pilot project and set in place some simple monitoring system to evaluate its effectiveness at the end of each year. However, if this was the pattern of development which did emerge, then in order to make any sensible judgement on the effectiveness of the project, similar monitoring activities would be needed on the year groups that were not in the project. This may in turn produce more tensions amongst the staff than the exercise is worth, and in which case the evaluation may be best left to the report presented by the tutor team concerned.

In practice of course one year group cannot be completely independent of the others and no-one would want to be. However, where there are differences between tutor teams in their degree of expertise and commitment, then senior management have the task of encouraging development in a co-ordinated way to make the best use for the school of the skills of all their staff.

## The needs of the year tutor group

To operate effectively as a pastoral team, a year tutor team needs certain kinds of support from the rest of the school and from the senior management team in particular. Time during the school day is obviously a significant resource, and it is clearly unreasonable to expect an effective tutor team to operate with only a minimal reduction on normal timetable. Some posts of responsibility in school can use time at the end of the day when the children have departed, but precisely because the pastoral team need time when the children are in school some timetable reduction is pretty well essential. Parts of the role in fact can be performed after school and parts, particularly parent liaison, have to be performed after school and often after five thirty.

The second general need is time to develop the group of form tutors and overall year tutor into a team, through the provision of in-service training opportunities relevant to their needs, and encouragement for them to meet to discuss pastoral matters. A part of team building is also insulation from sudden unplanned staff changes. Clearly from time to time there will be changes in tutor responsibilities, and sometimes senior management teams have to take a decision which is not generally welcomed by either the individual concerned or the team they are a part of. However, where staffing decisions to change tutor responsibilities are made in an arbitrary and apparently random fashion without consultation with the teams, staff morale will drop, the effectiveness of the team will also drop, and staff will begin to look for self-interest in the motivation of the senior managers concerned. Sometimes it is useful for expertise which may exist in one tutor team to be spread to another, which may mean moving some individuals. However, if this is the purpose of movement, then these purposes need to be spelled out to all those staff moving, and the nature of the improvements in practice expected in all teams affected should be made clear by the senior management team when the change occurs. When a new tutor moves into an existing team the year leader can suggest ways to help the new member learn the particular approaches and procedures adopted. For example, the year leader and one or two form tutors can 'team teach' one or two form periods, and particular materials or methods can be demonstrated. In this way the more experienced members of a tutor team can help to train teachers less experienced in the tutoring role, and the team develops the confidence to rely on each other rather than looking to the year leader to solve problems as they arise.

Year tutor teams also need sensitive support on the implementation of sanctions and disciplinary procedures, especially when they are grounded in whole school behaviour policies. A good general rule for senior managers is to intervene only when requested to so do by the tutors concerned.

Apart from support, an effectively functioning year tutor team needs recognition and approval from the school managers. Recognition can come in many ways, and a sensitive senior manager will be able to appreciate the most appropriate forms for the teams concerned. However, one form of recognition is support for the documentation of the achievements of the children in the year, including some of the performance indicators where appropriate, and support in finding space for tutor teams to report to management bodies and governors. The other major recognition which effective tutor teams appreciate very much is recognition of the educational values which underpin effective tutor work – recognition of the importance of building relationships with the children, aiming to increase the confidence of children, and the general contribution made to the academic achievement of the school by smoothly operating social links between students and the adult staff and between students and each other. Most senior management teams will be aware already of the need to support the team by giving recognition to the achievements of the team as a whole, not particular members of it.

# CHAPTER 9

# One School's Story – Establishing a Whole School Management Structure for Troubled Children in Inner-City Areas

## Introduction

The influence of the Committee of Enquiry (Elton) Report 'Discipline in Schools' (1989) is regarded as raising the profile of the pro-active whole school measures schools can take in creating and designing a school environment where all pupils and staff can operate. The committee was established in 1988:

'in response to concern about problems facing the teaching profession'.

At the time violent acts were reported seemingly on a daily basis in the newspapers and much 'public' concern was expressed about the lack of control in schools. The findings in the report however did not lend themselves to the general doom and gloom pervasive at the time. Indeed they showed that relations in schools between staff and pupils were generally good with only a small minority of pupils whose behaviour was consistently unsatisfactory. The significant majority of disruptive incidents were due to the sizeable numbers of petty as opposed to major incidents or interruptions occurring particularly in the classroom. As stated in the report:

'We find that most schools are on the whole well ordered. But even in well run schools minor disruption appears to be a problem...'.

In considering the effectiveness or otherwise of whole school approaches it is useful to review examples where a planned and purposeful approach has been designed and developed to address particular problems. Consequently, the remainder of this chapter concentrates on work undertaken in an all boys' high school where the need to develop such an approach occurred. The school operated from two sites set about a mile apart, and catered for the full range of pupils expectedly found in an urban setting.

**Background**

The writer joined the school used in this case study in April 1986, initially for a two year period, as part of an L.E.A. initiative.

The school had been recently inspected by an L.E.A. team, following violent incidents at school which had reached the press. One of its recommendations had been to create an extra post in school, taken by the writer. Its brief was to help increase the effectiveness of the pupil management systems particularly for pupils experiencing emotional and behavioural difficulties. A highly emotive phrase made in the Pastoral report had been picked up by the press. The Inspector wrote:

> Corridor behaviour was amongst the worst I have ever seen. Aggressive, violent behaviour appeared to be the norm. During the observation of three breaks I saw twenty-six aggressive incidents ranging from boys trying to throw one another off the balcony, to boys sprawled on the floor fighting.

At the time, the school was reported as being one of the most violent and aggressive in the country. In addition teacher union action was at the height of its 'popularity' and so considerable daily disruption was happening with many pupils being sent home.

The extra post had been titled 'advisory teacher', which was sometimes unhelpful, as it was very unspecific, especially as it was a full time post in one school. The title sets assumptions about 'watching rather than doing'. Interviews for the post were held in the holiday period, and as only two of the 110 staff saw the candidates, some mystery in the school surrounded the appointment.

It was interesting to talk to staff at the time about the school's image. Most, not surprisingly, rejected the public negative view. When considering the possible ways in which the advisory post could be developed, two distinct camps formed. One favoured the establishment of a unit for difficult and disaffected pupils, while the other (supported by the head teacher) wanted to see alternative strategies developed that supported staff and pupils in line with more progressive whole school methods.

These different perceptions on the possible role of a behaviour support unit were also related to the general divergence of views on the most appropriate style of response to disturbed behaviour from the school staff. Some teachers considered that the best response from the school staff was to consistently take a 'hard line' to those children showing disturbed behaviour, involving moving them to a behavioural unit, or through suspensions from school. Others felt that 'exporting the problem' did not give the school a viable means of building up effective systems for enforcing consistent standards of behaviour in schools. To be totally effective, such a system needed to have the support of all staff, particularly the head of school, and it would be virtually impossible to effect change unless the senior managers remained committed and supportive of the general in-school approach.These differences of view did not disappear overnight, and some divisions remained between the teaching staff over the next few years.

## Early contacts in school

The post was based in the lower school site and the first few weeks were spent in getting to know pupils and colleagues. From the outset staff were raising issues about the management of some pupils which often centred around the question: 'could you remove XXX from my lesson so that I can get on with teaching the rest of the class?'. Some staff clearly expected me to become the official school 'bouncer' patrolling corridors and swooping on any trouble while presumably being dressed in a superman costume. It was very important to dispel such an image early on because shared ownership rather than 'off loaded' responsibility is an important part of developing collective practice. One teacher requested that I stand outside the classroom and ensure that pupils lined up 'properly', others wanted to discuss and debate about what could and should be done.

I was appointed to the school from a teaching background in special and mainstream schools principally with troubled and troublesome pupils. I was therefore aware of the arguments relating to the establishment of a unit, and I personally adopted a firm and consistent line against such provision, both during the actual interview and in later discussions.

From earlier experiences, it was clear to me that establishing a behavioural unit was very unlikely to have a long term effect on the school's management of troubled children. This was for three main reasons:

1. The staff of the unit itself are under great pressure from managing the students' behaviour in the unit, and at the same time cannot support the student management procedures of the mainstream school.
2. Placing the students in a behavioural unit in fact becomes a self-fulfilling prophecy, in that when they realise their special treatment, their emerging identity as aggressive students is confirmed.
3. Once placed in the unit, it becomes very difficult for the students to move back to mainstream, and they are then very unlikely to learn to cope with formal classroom teaching situations.

## Initial approaches

My primary brief, then, was to work with teachers on management of pupils preferably within their own classes.

There were three interrelated factors incorporated into the introductory phase of the work. These were:

1. Firstly, to gain an understanding of the internal workings of the school's systems through undertaking some classroom teaching. In the first term I taught for fourteen out of twenty-five periods a week (through choice) to get to know the system from the inside and at the same time prove that I was a fully fledged teacher who could deliver the goods in the classroom.
2. Secondly, to identify any systems of support already used in school. This entailed considerable discussion with staff to piece together a network of information. It became clear that a developing pastoral system was being established with emphasis placed on the role of form tutors and heads of year. There was at the time little published information which indicated the clear delineation of roles or intent overall.
3. Thirdly, to collect some hard evidence as to central issues as identified by staff themselves. To this end a questionnaire was used to identify the key issues. A range of twenty-six commonly occurring behaviours were listed. The questions ranged from:
   — arrives late for lesson;
   — impedes others entering class;
   — uses abusive language;
   — is dominated by others.

Teachers were requested to tick those areas which concerned them most in relation to an individual pupil, a single group, several groups or with the majority of pupils within the classroom (it was suggested that staff complete the questionnaire with their 'worst' class in mind). Eighty-five questionnaires were given out to staff who taught or were based in the lower school with only twenty-one returned (or 24 per cent overall), an interesting figure on its own. The highest areas of concern (relating to individuals or small groups of pupils only) as recorded by staff using the questionnaire were as follows:
1. Arrives unprepared for lessons.
2. Slow to settle to class work.
3. Unable/unwilling to complete work tasks.
4. High level of classroom noise/arrives late for lesson (equal fourth).

The findings were then fed back to staff via several staff meetings and a consensus body of opinion confirmed that a united approach should be made by staff when teaching pupils who were experiencing difficulties. These results provided the evidence which then allowed such issues to be discussed in a rational and informed way throughout the school. The reaction was positive and certainly focussed attention onto managing and addressing basic issues of class administration. They also countered the view prevalent at the time that the school was an unstable and volatile place. In general these findings were similar to the ones identified in the Elton report that was published three years later. As Docking (1980) noted:

'...it seems that the daily stress, including problems that confront most teachers are more to do with fairly trivial but regular incidents of misbehaviour, such as talking and mucking around, than those with serious offences such as violence and verbal abuse'.

If undertaking a similar investigation again there would be a strong temptation to poll the views of pupils to gain a wider perception of the issues. Such an approach was undertaken by Newham Council in 1989 which found that nearly half of the 1,200 older secondary school pupils surveyed thought their teachers did not try hard enough to interest them and a quarter thought their teachers did not make them work hard enough.

## Responding to need

Two support mechanisms required development at one and the same time namely for pupils and for staff. Using the information gathered it was desirable to create clear guidance to advise and inform staff. Consequently, a written outline support system was produced which identified in linear terms where staff could go for advice and discussion to help ensure that some form of consistent and planned approach could be used. In essence this supported the subject and pastoral systems, with additional guidance becoming involved once key staff (heads of year/subject and form tutors) have had an involvement. A stage model moving staff from one level of support and intervention to another as part of an integrated managed approach also encouraged discussion and debate as to its value, effectiveness and purpose. It was in addition a starting point in the process of meeting both staff and pupil needs.

In practice the process involved the identification of need, planning to address the problem and evaluation of programme. Staff were required to use the system and if the response did not produce the desired result then a wider support base was used in a planned and systematic way. The elements linked together and in effect it became a filter system of support that encouraged greater contact and discussion between subject and pastoral areas. In a broad sense the support structure was strongly allied to the Warnock stages of intervention although tightly focussed on actual schools structures.

It became clear that there were within the school a group of pupils who did present considerable challenges to the management and general discipline structure. Although a separate pupil 'unit' was not created, opportunities were established whereby certain pupils in years 7 to 9 were taught as a distinct group for one or two lessons in a week.

These lessons were specifically targeted on pupils already identified through the support system structure as being the most demanding and difficult across a number of subject areas.

During the first term contact was made with the central support service for emotionally and behaviourally disturbed pupils who had previously worked within the school in a sessional and generally unfocussed way. It was considered advantageous to re-define their involvement and to concentrate attention onto the small group of identified pupils. These pupils found it hard to manage themselves in the classroom and were therefore seen as potentially the most difficult to control. The work undertaken concentrated on teaching these pupils alternative methods of coping and managing themselves more effectively particularly in the classroom situation. This form of group work continued for several academic years guiding pupils into a stage model approach of tackling problematic situations that they commonly found hard to manage.

While the general feel of the school was being assimilated and day to day routines began to become established, other practical matters presented themselves. Although no separate unit as such was created, there was a need to develop a resource base to facilitate both the pupil group work and an appropriate area for meetings and equipment (video, computer and general support materials). A classroom was identified as an appropriate venue and although a couple of later moves to other rooms became necessary it proved its worth over time. By the end of the first term a number of initial objectives of the policy development had been achieved.

Regrettably, shortly after the start of the second term a fatal stabbing occurred in school. The deep scar that such a tragedy left on many teachers and perhaps more so on the pupils who witnessed the death should never be underestimated. The purpose of this case study is to describe the establishment of effective pupil management techniques over the next few years, not to focus on the immediate consequences of such an extreme form of violent behaviour. The subsequent enquiry into events surrounding the death started in 1987, while the report itself was finally published by the L.E.A. as the MacDonald Report in 1990.

Aside from coping and dealing with such a tragedy it was essential to continue to build on the need to share information with staff on alternative methods to manage pupils. The schools in-service training programme continued, and a number of information sheets were produced, to help communication with all staff. One particularly useful and interesting training exercise centred on good behaviour and discipline in classrooms. The activity involved teachers firstly, identifying all the aspects of pupil behaviours that they considered constituted difficult and demanding behaviour. Secondly, planning how to address such problems. The standard group work format was used with firstly individual identification within a small group situation (brainstorming) then leading to full group discussion of the range of problems.

Eleven broadly based problem areas were identified ranging from:

— pupil organisation (lesson change-overs);
— authority refusal;
— negative attitude and/or poor attention;
— verbal – physical disruption, etc.

In all, seventy-one different problem behaviours were identified by the whole staff group. The question was then to consider how such behaviour could be managed within the school. Interestingly, a total of 126 possible solutions were identified by staff which then again led to a valuable and informative exchange across subject and pastoral areas. This information was reproduced to form the basis of further staff meetings.

A regular cycle of staff training programmes were offered to groups and individual teachers to respond to the changing set of pupil needs identified in the school, e.g. managing a difficult year group or conflict management together with commercially available training systems. It was essential to balance the support and guidance to staff with a responsive and relevant intervention process to pupils. However, such a pupil centred approach can cause a 'backlash' in the staffroom unless the process is seen to work in the general favour of the school as a whole. The system must also be accepted at senior management levels before any credibility can be afforded to it. A broad range of structures were used that developed according to the age and needs of the pupils as follows:

1. Contracting between school, home, pupil and other significant adults. As in all contracts, negotiation plays a key part in the process and pupils were included from the outset in the design and formulation of the actual contents.

2. Community placements and extended work experience programmes tended to be used with Y10 and Y11 pupils as a part of a planned programmed approach to positively enhance and build up a pupil's limited self worth and confidence. A number of neighbourhood primary schools were used with pupils attending for fixed times in the week as additional helpers.

3. Negotiated timetables often removed the potential for a problem to arise as pupils were able to move between groups with minimal disruption as agreement would have been sought and given from the teachers concerned.

4. Maximising the use of all external and internal resources and support systems available to the school (e.g. educational psychologists and advisory teachers). These can often provide further resources for managing pupil behaviours.

5. Monitoring systems that fully involved pupils in both the design and practicable application of report forms. Considerable use was made of

negotiation directly with pupils to identify what they felt the problem was and more importantly what could be done to help. By and large pupils were able to identify where and why things went wrong in many situations. They also could pinpoint the actions and reactions they produced which could lead to further difficulty. Behaviours were measured and recorded by staff with targets set with pupils.

6. Home school liaison was given considerable attention particularly for the more disruptive or difficult pupils. These arrangements were part of a planned and co-ordinated school response and, although labour intensive, did produce positive results. This was particularly so when issues of discipline (visiting as a result of poor behaviour) were dealt with separately from regular reviewing and discussion of general progress and support. Pupils were always encouraged to attend such reviews.

7. Regular meetings with pupils to review support arrangements provided the link between guidance and control. This necessitated close collaboration with Heads of Years to collate and sift through information, reports and general comments that would filter through on behaviour, attitude and work in school.

8. Creation of specific lessons for identified pupils on the teaching of pupil self management skills linked to the positive elements of assertiveness training.

9. Working directly with targeted pupils by providing direct teaching support in lessons where difficulties were likely to occur. The essential element of any support or intervention system centred on the effectiveness of the communication involved. This relates to both teachers and pupil contact. Interpreting situations and offering alternative ways of responding particularly to difficult pupils proved to be a most useful exercise.

## Conclusions

The success or otherwise of this attempt to develop a whole school approach to the management of difficult pupils in a high school setting can be judged by a number of measures for example: exclusions from school, attendance rates, parental complaints against other pupils' behaviours, use and frequency of internal school sanctions (detentions), etc. The additional post created by the L.E.A. in the study school, was to the author's knowledge fairly unique. In addition it was funded as a direct response to a particular need being identified following a school's inspection. Many of the interventions and support strategies described here were developed to address the particular situation. The additional post was discontinued five years after its establishment.

It may be regarded in today's market place economy which is so much in evidence in schools that such a specific and possibly specialist teaching post is a luxury and expense very few schools could or would want to establish. The creation of a successful whole school approach is heavily reliant upon commitment from the schools' senior managers who must be mindful of the indicators identified in league tables now available to parents to compare 'performance' between schools. Time is often in short supply in schools and therefore a balance needs to be struck between dealing with daily misdemeanours and the need for establishing clear and objective behaviour management policies that are linked to effective practice that may lead to a calmer, rational and purposeful environment for both teachers and pupils.

# References

Arora, C.M.J. (1989) 'Bullying – Action and Intervention', *Pastoral Care in Education,* **Vol.7**, No.3, pp.44-47.

Arora, C.M.J. and Thompson, D.A. (1987) *'Defining Bullying for a Secondary School',* Educational and Child Psychology, **Vol.4**, No.304, pp.110-112.

Arora, R.K. and Duncan, C.G. (eds) (1986) *Multi-Cultural Education: Towards Good Practice.* London: Routledge.

Arora, T. (1994) 'Is there any point in trying to reduce bullying in secondary schools?, *Educational Psychology in Practice,* in press.

Asher, S.R. and Coie, J.D. (1990) *Peer Rejection in Childhood.* Cambridge: Cambridge University Press.

Ball, S.J. and Goodson, I.F. (eds) (1985) *Teachers' Lives and Careers.* Lewes: Falmer Press.

Banks, N. (1993) 'Identity work with children', *Journal of Educational and Child Psychology,* **Vol.10**, No.3, pp.43-46.

Besag, V.E. (1989) *Bullies and Victims in Schools.* Milton Keynes: Open University Press.

Best, R., Jarvis, C. and Ribbins, P. (eds) (1984) *Perspectives on Pastoral Care.* London: Heinemann Educational Books.

Blatchford, P. and Sharp, S. (eds) (1993) *Understanding and Changing School Playground Behaviour.* London: Routledge.

Blatchford, P. (1989) *Playtime in the Primary School.* Windsor: NFER-Nelson.

Boulton, M. and Smith, P.K. (1986) 'Rough and Tumble Play in Children: Environmental Influences', *Playworld Journal,* **Vol.1**, pp.15-17.

Bulman, L. (1984) 'The Relationship Between the Pastoral Curriculum, The Academic Curriculum, and the Pastoral Programme', *Pastoral Care in Education.* **Vol.2**, pp.107-113. Oxford: N.A.P.C.E./Basil Blackwell.

Cassdagli, P. and Gobey, F. (1990) *Only Playing Miss!* Stoke on Trent: Trentham Books/Professional Development Foundation.

Central Independent Television (1990) *Sticks and Stones.* Video, available from the Community Unit, Central Television, Broad Street, Birmingham BI 2JP.

Central Independent Television (1990) *The Trouble with Tom.* Video, available from the Community Unit, Central Television, Broad Street, Birmingham BI 2JP.

Cohen, P. (1992) '"It's Racism What Dunnit": Hidden Narratives in Theories of Racism'. Paper in Donald and Rattansi (eds) op. cit. pp.62-103.

Cole, R. (1977) 'Teachers' *Views on Bullying in Schools',* unpublished MSc (Educational Psychology) dissertation, Department of Education, University of Sheffield Library.

Dean, J. (1985) *Managing the Secondary School.* Beckenham: Croom Helm.

Dickinson, P. (1982) 'Facts and Figures: Some Myths', in Tierney, J. (ed), op.cit. pp.58-85.

Docking, J. (1980) *Control and Discipline in Schools – perspectives and approaches*. London: Harper and Row.

Donald, J. and Rattansi, A. (1992) *Race, Culture and Difference*. London: Sage/The Open Universlty.

Duncan, C. (1988) *Pastoral Care: An Anti-Racist/Multi-Cultural Perspective*. Oxford: Blackwell.

Elton, R. (1989) *Discipline in Schools – Report of the Committee of Enquiry*. London: DfE/HMSO.

Erwin, P. (1993) *Friendship and Peer Relations in Children*. Chichester: Wiley.

Everaard, K.B. and Morris, G. (1990) *Effective School Management*, 2nd edition. London: Paul Chapman.

Everaard, K.B. (1989) 'Organisational Development in Educational Institutions', in Entwhistle, N. (ed) *Handbook of Educational Ideas and Practices*. London: Routledge.

Forde, S., Lesnah, H. and McLean, Z. (1988) *The Real McCoy – The A-Z of Black People in History*. London: A.L.B.S.U.

Foster, P., Arora, C.M.J. and Thompson, D.A. (1990) 'A Whole School Approach to Bullying', *Pastoral Care in Education*, **Vol.8**, No.3, pp.13-17.

Foster, P. and Thompson, D.A. (1991) 'Bullying – Towards a Non-violent Sanctions Policy', in Smith, P.K. and Thompson, D.A. (eds) *Practical Approaches to Bullying*. London: Fulton.

Gaine, C. (1987) *No Problem Here: A Practical Approach to Education and Race in White Schools*. London: Hutchinson.

Galloway, D. (1989) 'Special Educational Needs and Pastoral Care', in Ramasut, A. (ed) *Whole School Approaches to Special Needs*. Lewes: Falmer Press.

Galvin, P., Mercer, S. and Costa, P. (1989) *Building a Better Behaved School*. Harlow: Longman.

Giddens, A. (1989) *Sociology*. Cambridge: Polity Press.

Gill, D. and Levidow, L. (eds) (1987) *Anti-Racist Science Teaching*. London: Free Association Books.

Gillborn, D. (1990) Race, *Ethnicity and Education: Teaching and Learning in Multi-ethnic Schools*. London: Unwin Hyman.

Hammersley, M. (1984) 'Staff Room News', in Hargreaves, A. and Woods, P. (eds) *Classrooms and Staff Rooms: The Sociology of Teachers and Teaching*. Milton Keynes: Open University Press.

Handy, C.B. and Aitken, R. (1986) *Understanding Schools as Organisations*. Harmondsworth: Penguin.

Hargreaves, A. and Woods, P. (eds) (1984) *Classrooms and Staff Rooms: The Sociology of Teachers and Teaching*. Milton Keynes: Open University Press.

Her Majesty's Inspectorate (1977) *Ten Good Schools*. London: DES/HMSO.

Higgins, C. (1994) 'Improving the School Ground Environment as an Anti-bully-ing Strategy', in Smith, P.K. and Sharp, S. op. cit.

Hopkins, D. (ed) (1986) *In-Service Training and Educational Development: An International Survey.* Beckenham: Croom Helm.

Imich, A. and Jefferies, K. (1989) 'Management of Lunchtime Behaviour', *Support for Learning,* **Vol.4**, pp.46-52.

INSET Workshops for Schools ( 1989).
1. Whole-school policy for Health and Sex Education.
2. Whole-school approaches to Multi-cultural Education.
3. Developing an Equal Opportunities Policy on Gender.
Basingstoke: Macmillan Education.

Jones, J. (1988) 'Pervading Themes and Issues in the Management of Staff Development', *British Journal of In-service Education,* **Vol.14,** No. 3, pp. 202-19.

Kriedler, W.J. (1984) *Creative Conflict Resolution.* Illinois: Goodyear Press.

Kumar, A. (1985) *The Heartstone Odyssey,* Allied House Publications (Allied House, First Floor, Longden Court, Spring Gardens, Buxton, Derbyshire SK17 6BZ).

Lieberman, A. (ed) ( 1990) *Schools as Collaborative Cultures: Creating the Future Now.* Lewes: Falmer Press.

Lieberman, A. and Miller, L. ( 1 990) 'The Social Realities of Teaching', in Lieberman, A. (ed), op. cit.

Little, J.W. (1990) 'Teachers as Colleagues', in Lieberman, A. (ed), op. cit.

MacDonald, I. (1990) *'Murder in the Playground – the report of the MacDonald enquiry into racism and racial violence in Manchester schools'.* London: Longsight Press.

Maines, B. and Robinson, G. (1993) *Stamp Out Bullying.* Bristol: Lame Duck Publishing.

Maxime, J.E. (1993) 'The ethnographic dimension of race and its mental health and educational implications', *Journal of Educational and Child Psychology,* **Vol.10**, No.3, pp.28-38.

Miller, A. (1994) 'Staff Culture, Boundary Maintenance and Successful "Behavioural Interventions" in Primary Schools', *Research Papers in Education,* **Vol.9**, No.1.

Nabuzoka, D., Whitney, I., Smith, P.K. and Thompson, D. (1993) 'Bullying and Children with Special Educational Needs', in Tattum, D. (ed) *Understanding and Managing Bullying.* London: Heinemann.

National Curriculum Council (1989) *The National Curriculum and Whole Curriculum Planning: Preliminary Guidance Circular No.6. York:* National Curriculum Council. .

137

National Curriculum Council (1993). *'Spiritual and Moral Development'*. York: National Curriculum Council.

Nias, J. (1985) 'Reference Groups in Primary Teaching', in Ball, S.J. and Goodson, I.F. (eds) (1985) *Teachers' Lives and Careers*. Lewes: Falmer Press.

Nixon, J. (1985) *A Teacher's Guide to Multi-Cultural Education*. Oxford: Blackwell.

Olweus, D. (1978) *Aggression in the Schools: Bullies and Whipping Boys*. Washington DC: Hemisphere.

Olweus, D. (1979) 'Stability of Aggressive Reaction Patterns in Males: A Review', *Psychological Bulletin,* **Vol.86**, No.4, pp.852-875.

Olweus, D. (1993) *Bullying Among School Children: Intervention and Prevention*. Oxford: Blackwell.

Olweus, D. (1989) 'Bully Victim Problems Among School Children: Basic Facts and Effects of a School Based Intervention Programme', in Riubin, K. and Peper, D. (eds) *The Development and Treatment of Childhood Aggression*. Hillsdale, New Jersey: Erlbaum.

Philips, D. (1989) 'Teachers' Attitudes to Pupils with Learning Difficulties', in Ramasut, A. (ed) *Whole School Approaches to Special Needs*. Lewes: Falmer Press.

Ponterotto, J.G. and Pedersen, P.B. (1993) *Preventing Prejudice – A Guide for Counsellors and Educators*. London: Sage.

Quicke, J. (1985) *Disability in Modern Children's Fiction*. Beckenham: Croom Helm.

Rattansi, A. (1992) 'Changing the Subject? Racism, Culture and Education', paper in Donald, J., and Rattansi, A., *Race, Culture and Difference*. London: Sage/The Open University.

Reynolds, D. (1989) 'Effective Schooling for Children with Special Educational Needs. Research and its implications', in Ramasut (ed) *Whole School Approaches to Special Needs*. Lewes: Falmer Press.

Rigby, K. and Slee, P. (1993) 'Children's Attitudes Towards Victims', in Tattum, D. (ed) *Understanding and Managing Bullying*. London: Heinemann.

Ross, C. and Ryan, A. (1989) *Can I Stay in Today Miss?* – Improving the School Playground. The Islington Schools' Environmental Project, Islington Education Department.

Rowland, E. (1993) 'Bullying: A Developing Tradition of Research and Management', in Tattum, D. (ed) *Understanding and Managing Bullying*. London: Heinemann.

Sharp, S. (1993) 'Lunchtime Supervisor Training in the UK: An Overview', in Blatchford, P. and Sharp, S. (eds) *Understanding and Changing School Playground Behaviour*. London: Routledge.

138

Sharp, S. (1994) 'The effects of bullying on pupil learning, attendance and well-being – reasons for intervention'. Paper presented at Annual Conference of the British Psychological Society.

Sharp, S. (1994) 'Barriers to parental involvement'. Unpublished paper, Division of Education, Sheffield University.

Sharp, S., Sellars, A. and Cowie, H. (1994) 'Time to listen – setting up a peer counselling service in a school', in press, *Pastoral Care in Education,* **Vol.12**.

Sheat, L. (1991) *How to Improve Our School Grounds*. School Grounds Design Pack, Department of Landscape, University of Sheffield.

Smith, D.J. and Tomlinson, S. (1989) *The School Effect – A Study of Multi-Racial Comprehensives*. London: Policy Studies Institute.

Smith, G. (1994) 'The Safer Schools – Safer Cities Bullying Project'. Paper presented at Annual Conference of the British Psychological Society.

Smith, P.K. and Sharp, S. (1994) *School Bullying and How To Cope With It*. London: Routledge.

Smith, P.K. and Thompson, D.A. (1991) 'Dealing with Bully-Victim Problems in the UK', in Smith, P.K. and Thompson D.A. (eds) *Practical Approaches to Bullying*. London: Fulton .

Smith, P.K. and Thompson, D.A. (eds) (1991) *Practical Approaches to Bullying*. London: Fulton.

Stephenson, P. and Smith, D. (1989) *'Bullying in the Junior School'*, in Tattum, D.P. and Lane, D.A. (eds) Bullying in Schools. Stoke-on-Trent: Trentham Press.

Swann, M. (1985) *Education for All: A Final Report of the Committee of Enquiry into the Education of Children from Ethnic Minority Groups*. London: HMSO, Cmnd 9453.

The DES (1990) 'The Outdoor Classroom: Educational Use, Landscape Design and Management in School Grounds', *Building Bulletin*, **Vol.71**. HMSO.

The National Association for Pastoral Care in Education Pastoral Care in Education, N.A.P.C.E. (c/o Education Department, University of Warwick, Coventry CV4 7AL).

Thompson, D.A. and Arora, T. (1991) 'Why Do Children Bully? An Evaluation of the Long-Term Effectiveness of a Whole-school Policy to Minimize Bullying', Pastoral Care in Education, **Vol.9**, No.1, pp.8-12.

Thompson, D.A., Whitney, I. and Smith, P.K. (1994) 'Bullying of Children with Special Needs in Mainstream Schools', Support for Learning, in press.

Tierney, J. (ed) (1982) *Race, Migration and Schooling*. London: Holt, Reinhart and Whinston.

Trimmingham, C. (1994) *Bullying of Statemented Children in Mainstream Schools – Parents' Perceptions of the Issues'*. Unpublished MSc (Educational Psychology) dissertation, Department of Education, University of Sheffield Library.

# INDEX

140

involving pupils, 104-106

leadership and management, 34-36, 111, 122-123
Macdonald Report, 130
managing very challenging pupils, 129-132
mentoring, 93
method of shared concern, 81-82
monitoring and review, 42-44, 108-111, 132

National Curriculum, 55
negotiated timetable, 131

peer support for teachers, 87-90
playground environment, 82-84
prejudice and harassment, 2-3
process of policy development, 10, 101-102
difficulties in, 112
professional isolation, 87
provision for children with special needs, 22-24
public relations, 30-31

rules, 2
limitations of, 8-9
social, 4-5, 8

sanctions, 75-82, 108
Sheffield Anti-Bullying Project, 96-101
staff behaviour, 49
staff responsibilities, 117-119
supervision
management of, 74-75
support for, 72
to reduce victimisation, 70-72
training for, 74-75, 95
Swann Report, 54

tensions, 9, 16-17, 20-23
training, 90-93

evaluation of, 95
for home visiting, 120-121
for supervision, 95
transition management, 36-37
values, 1, 37

Warnock, 22
whole school project management group, 64-65, 86, 92
withdrawal groups, 130-131

year teams, 116